AMERICAN LIT
101

FROM **NATHANIEL HAWTHORNE** TO
HARPER LEE AND **NATURALISM** TO
MAGICAL REALISM, AN ESSENTIAL GUIDE
TO **AMERICAN WRITERS** AND **WORKS**

BRIANNE KEITH

Avon, Massachusetts

Published by
Adams Media, a division of F+W Media, Inc.
57 Littlefield Street, Avon, MA 02322. U.S.A.
www.adamsmedia.com

ISBN 10: 1-4405-9968-8
ISBN 13: 978-1-4405-9968-2
eISBN 10: 1-4405-9969-6
eISBN 13: 978-1-4405-9969-9

Printed in the United States of America.

10 9 8 7 6 5 4 3 2 1

Cover design by Michelle Kelly.
Cover images: Emily Dickinson © Public Domain via Wikimedia Commons;
Getty Images/ivan-96; ilbusca.

This book is available at quantity discounts for bulk purchases.
For information, please call 1-800-289-0963.

DEDICATION

To Thoreau, who kindled the flame,
and to Brad Dean, who fed it

ACKNOWLEDGMENTS

Writing a book takes an enormous amount of work and support. I want to thank all of the people who supported me while writing—in particular, Bill, Richard, and Scott, whose steady encouragement kept me afloat. Thanks to my parents, and to K, for educating me in all senses of the word. I want to thank Peter Archer for his careful and diligent editorial work, Eileen Mullan for her cheerful guidance and support, and the rest of the Adams Media team for their work putting this book together. Lastly, I want to thank Katie Corcoran Lytle for once again graciously pulling me onto another fantastic project.

CONTENTS

INDEX   248

INTRODUCTION

A friend who's a historian once told me, "Literary scholars argue so viciously because nothing is at stake." What a statement! (I can hear an army of proverbial swords being drawn in the distance.) So what did he mean?

It may seem that literature has no bearing on our day-to-day lives, but it certainly does. Writers and literature express a shared understanding of a time and place in history—it is through their voices that we have an opportunity to gain a greater understanding of ourselves and our world.

Nineteenth-century readers of Mark Twain's *Adventures of Huckleberry Finn*, for instance, might have recognized Huckleberry's dialect in their own neighborhood boys shouting in the streets, just as we hear our own voices in television shows and movies now. Aristotle said that art can purge us of our emotions as they are mirrored back to us. The same is true of literature. We understand the beliefs and values of our age as they are reflected back to us by the words and actions of the characters we read in a book, or the pitch and tone of a voice in a poem. Through this understanding we can find solidarity with each other, and also find the words to define the differences among us—all composing the fabric of our lives.

What is American literature and how does it differ from any other literature? American literature is, simply, literature written by Americans! It is the literature that tells the stories, attitudes, and beliefs of Americans from their beginnings to the writers of today.

In many ways American literature is a coming-of-age story (or the beginning of one—we're still young!). Writers of the colonial age documented their early experiences of survival in diaries, poems, and captivity narratives; writers of the revolutionary era documented the birth pangs that come with the founding of a country in pamphlets, letters, and political texts; early literary writers strove to create a uniquely American literature as it sought to establish its literary independence from Britain.

Writers of the nineteenth century documented the push and pull of a country coming together under a national culture of optimism and hope, then tearing itself apart during the Civil War. The late nineteenth and twentieth centuries saw writers trying to find humor in the forces of an expanding country devastated by war with the battle scars to prove it.

In the "waste land" that followed, American writers showed their resilience—writers endured but also flourished! Some of the most innovative work was produced in the twentieth century. Writers responded to the call to "make it new" in a surge of creativity that put into motion new forms, new tones, and new themes that defined and pushed American literature forward. Writers once again found the creative optimism, present since the founding of the country, through defiance and nonconformity (the bread and butter of the American culture!). That optimism still survives in the writers capturing their difficult journeys toward identity in assimilation in American literature.

American literature reflects the endurance of the American spirit and surge of creative forces at play in American culture. In this book you'll learn about the various authors, works, and literary movements that make up American literature. Sit back and get ready for a wild ride!

Chapter 1

Literature of the New World

Early American literature has a lot to teach about the lives, hopes, wishes, and values of the early colonists who settled America. The intensity of their religious devotion was reflected in their poetry, their extreme suffering in the New World ran deep throughout their personal diaries and captivity narratives, and their belief in their religious experiment blazed through their sermons. The sermons and poems produced during this era were united by an attempt to keep faith strong and remind colonists of their purpose in the face of a harsh and harrowing new experience trying to survive in the New World.

Alongside these early Puritan settlers were other groups of people, too—people who came for entirely different reasons than religious refuge. Some came to seek adventure, some came to better their economic status, some came to escape imprisonment at home. And of course, there were the people already living here—the Native Americans. All of their lives, stories, and voices are part of the fabric of early American literature. In this chapter, you will read selections that reflect their stories and voices and the changing modes of understanding the world that were developing almost as soon as the first English settlers established their colonies on the Eastern Seaboard in the early seventeenth century.

EXPLORING AMERICA

Explorers' Accounts and the "Contact Zone"

When two people meet for the first time, they exchange a lot of information. Think about when you first meet someone, especially someone from a different culture. Quite naturally, your eyes automatically scan the person's appearance, dress, and gestures. The larger the differences between your cultures, the more information you will need to process.

So imagine when the natives of South and North America spotted the early European explorers sailing toward their shores in huge, multisail ships that were so different from their own. Talk about information overload!

FIRST IMPRESSIONS

When European explorers met with the natives of these new continents, there was much more at stake than a simple exchange of information—for all parties. The Europeans arrived with an agenda: to conquer new territory to call their own. This was a clash of epic proportions, and no one would be left unchanged. The natives' agenda? To survive.

(Mis)Interpretations

One literary scholar, Mary Louise Pratt, has a term for these types of interactions where cultures meet and a power struggle ensues. She calls this the "contact zone." When two cultures meet, the records of their exchanges are fraught with the attitudes, beliefs, and agendas of each culture. In these contact zones, Pratt claims, there is much at stake, and the texts must be read carefully for clues of dominance and submission, power and oppression. For a *complete* history, the voices from both sides are needed.

When Bernal Díaz del Castillo (1492–1584) wrote his *The True History of the Conquest of New Spain*, he certainly was staking *his* claim in the history of Spanish conquest of Mexico. Diaz, who spent most of his life in the West Indies, accompanied both Hernando de Soto and Hernán Cortés on expeditions to lay claim to new land. These bloody missions left an indelible mark on Díaz, who later said he could not sleep through the night. At the age of eighty-four, blind and deaf, Díaz sat down to write his story. In the *True History*, he tells of how the Aztecs presented the Spaniards with gifts:

> The [Aztec] prince Quintalbor…bore…presents…The first was a disk in the shape of a sun, as big as a cartwheel and made of a very fine gold … There was another larger disk of brightly shining silver in the shape of a moon, with other figures on it, and this was worth a great deal for it was very heavy … Quintalbor also brought back [a] helmet full of small grains of gold, just as they come from the mines and worth three thousand pesos. The gold in the helmet was worth more than twenty thousand pesos to us, because it proved to us that there were good mines in the country.

In this passage we can see that Díaz, as with many other Spanish soldiers of the conquest, had one interest in mind: what he stood to gain after the Aztecs were conquered. In this simple exchange of gifts, Díaz was less interested in what the Aztecs meant by presenting these gifts and more interested in what the gifts suggested about the presence of gold in the country, and subsequently, the riches they could keep for themselves and send back home to Spain.

How would Quintalbor's account of this exchange read? Very differently one could suppose! What did Quintalbor mean by presenting the gifts? What did the gifts mean to the Aztec culture? What message did the gifts send?

If Quintalbor *had* written an account of the dominance, destruction, and enslavement of his people by Díaz and his fellow conquistadores, his text would be an example of *autoethnography* (don't get too distracted by the term). In an autoethnographic text, an author tells and connects his or her own story to the wider historical context of which it is a part. Quintalbor would in a sense "recapture" his story and the story of the Aztecs from Díaz's account, which has made its way down in history as the story of the "winner."

What Does It Mean?

Autoethnography is made up of the prefix *auto*, meaning "self," and the word *ethnography*, which refers to the scientific description of the customs of individuals and cultures.

In fact, natives of the New World *did* eventually create their own accounts of their first encounters with European conquerors. Within a few dozen years of the arrival of the Spanish, Aztecs began to learn the Spanish language and Roman alphabet, and in their own literature they documented the horrors of their captivity and destruction. Perhaps the earliest account is this Nahuatl (Aztec) poem from 1528:

Broken spears lie in the roads;
we have torn our hair in grief.
The houses are roofless now, and their walls
are red with blood.

ACCOUNTS OF THE NEW WORLD

Díaz's account was just one of many explorers' accounts of the New World. Of course, we all know of Columbus, who in 1492 "sailed the ocean blue" and his texts. And thanks to the invention of the printing press in the mid-1400s, we have a number of other texts, including formal statements to the kings and queens financing the expeditions back in Europe, letters, diary entries, and narratives that survive from this age telling the stories of these "voyages of discovery." It's important to remember that these texts all had a purpose: They were written to influence policymakers back home, to convince financiers that their investments in these voyages were successful and bearing fruit; and some were more personal, to provide firsthand testimony of the destruction and horror explorers bore witness to.

Bartolomé de Las Casas (1474–1566)

De Las Casas is an example of an explorer who came to regret his actions in the New World. He came to the New World from Spain in 1502 on a mission to Hispaniola and later wrote about his exploitations in an effort to reform brutal Spanish policy overseas. He wrote in his *The Very Brief Relation of the Devastation of the Indies* how "Christians, with their horses and swords and pikes began to carry out massacres and strange cruelties" against natives, and described in detail practices that would horrify readers today. De Las Casas wrote that natives' weapons were "weak" and "because of this, the wars of Indians against each other were little more than games played by children," giving a glimpse into the world that the Spanish destroyed.

NATIVE AMERICAN LITERATURE

Oral Traditions

Using the term "Native American literature" to describe the stories of natives of the New World is kind of a misnomer since natives of the New World didn't have written traditions. There was no established alphabet by which native tribes across the continents wrote down their stories.

Native cultures had *oral traditions*. A story would be passed down from generation to generation, spoken by a storyteller, usually around a fire at night. Stories would change as each storyteller put his or her own spin on the stories with gestures, tone, and other alterations to minor story details. The main part of the story would remain intact, though, but would be given new life and meaning with each generation's storytellers.

Some Written Traditions

Some cultures did have forms of written traditions—Aztecs used intricate arrangements of shells to make records, and other cultures used hieroglyphics and other pictographic drawings to record important stories and messages.

Moreover, there was no common language shared by native nations across the Americas at the time of the Europeans' arrival. In fact, no unified Native American culture existed at that time or at any other. Hundreds of tribes and nations ranged across the continents and organized their societies in different ways. They had different economic and political systems, different linguistic structures, and different customs. More organized tribal societies coexisted beside hunter-gatherer societies. It was a genuine mix of cultures.

Where Europeans had comedies, tragedies, sonnets, and lyrics, native cultures developed their own storytelling forms. Here are a few representative types.

TRICKSTER TALES

Trickster tales were common across Native American cultures. The "trickster" is usually a rowdy, childlike prankster who causes trouble wherever he goes. He doesn't care to play by the rules and doesn't have much respect for authority. He has magical abilities and can change gender on a whim—usually to avoid getting caught or to cause mischief. The trickster was commonly associated with an animal. In the West he was a coyote, in the Southeast he was a rabbit, and in the northern Great Plains he was a spider. The trickster is a troublemaker, but he also carries a powerful message: Through the disorder he causes, he pushes people to think about what they value and know. Tales about a familiar trickster character were usually strung together into "cycles" of different episodes.

Coyote and the Fish

In a Clatsop Chinook trickster tale, the trickster figure Coyote learns certain fishing taboos to follow in order to catch and keep fish in the rivers. After each failure, he consults his excrement, which reveals another secret about how to properly catch, cut, and cook fish.

CREATION STORIES

Like Europeans, Native American cultures had their own stories about how they came to be. Native American creation stories helped cultures understand their role on Earth. The stories were usually set in nature and had anthropomorphic characters, supernatural events, and complicated storylines. Many native cultures also had stories of a "great flood," just like the Judeo-Christian traditions (as well as other religious traditions around the world).

STORIES OF RITUALS

Like any culture, Native American cultures each had specific rituals to welcome new life, celebrate rites of passage, and bury the dead. Information about conducting important rituals was shared through song, dance, and music. Stories about how the rituals came to be were often woven into long song cycles.

Mojave Song Cycles

One Mojave song cycle, composed of 525 songs, tells a creation story. The song cycle is sung over several days after someone dies. The cycle helps the deceased on his or her journey in the afterlife.

CAPTIVITY NARRATIVES

Early Literature in the New World

One of the earliest genres to emerge in American literature is the captivity narrative. Captivity narratives tell the experiences of a person being held captive by an enemy, and are usually distinguished by the author's disapproval of the captor's beliefs or customs. These narratives tell of gruesome events and the strength and courage taken to overcome them. Some of the earliest examples of captivity narratives in American literature were written by women. For this reason, these narratives often give us fascinating glimpses into women's experiences during the early days of the colonists.

NATIVE AMERICAN INVOLVEMENT

It didn't take long for things to deteriorate between Native Americans and the first English colonists. Within sixty years, the friendly contract that the *Mayflower* pilgrims established with surrounding Native American tribes was broken, and war broke out. When colonists executed three of Metacomet's Wampanoag tribesmen in Plymouth, Massachusetts, Metacomet, or King Philip (his adopted English name), waged a war against the colonists. He and his tribesmen tore through settlements burning houses and killing men, women, and children, and took dozens of colonists hostage. These attacks became known as the First Indian War, or King Philip's War.

Mary Rowlandson, the wife of a Puritan minister, was one of the many hostages taken during these attacks. She wrote about her captivity in *A Narrative of the Captivity and Restoration of Mrs. Mary*

Rowlandson. In her narrative she describes in rich detail the events of the attack and her three-month captivity. She tells how her attackers tore through her village with bullets that "seemed to fly like hail," slashing and disemboweling men before her eyes. One bullet caught her and her child:

> One [bullet] went through my side, and the same (as would seem) through the bowels and hand of my dear child in my arms.

With her child in her arms, she was forced away from the scene, to walk 150 miles with her captors through the thick forests of North America, away from life as she knew it. Nine days into the trek her child died; two other children were later sold to different tribes.

The interesting thing about these captivity narratives is that they often show the complicated relationships between captor and captive. Rowlandson watched the merciless slaughter of her brother-in-law:

> No sooner were we out of the house, but my brother-in-law (being wounded, in defending the house, in or near the throat) fell down dead, whereat the Indians scornfully shouted, and hallowed, and were presently upon him, stripping off his clothes.

But she would later find sympathy and grace with the people who so brutally killed her relatives. She describes how, when she was wild with hunger, a Native American woman offered her some food:

> But I was fain to go and look after something to satisfy my hunger, and going among the wigwams, I went into one and there found a squaw who showed herself very kind to me, and gave me a piece of bear . . . I have sometime seen bear baked very handsomely

among the English, and some like it, but the thought that it was bear made me tremble. But now that was savory to me that one would think was enough to turn the stomach of a brute creature.

While the thought of eating bear once made Rowlandson "tremble," she now found it "savory" in the face of real hunger. Rowlandson was eventually ransomed by her husband and set free three months after her capture, but clearly she was a new person. Her narrative documents a woman whose ordeal continually tested and restored her faith in God, and expanded her courage, even down to the food she was willing to eat.

The Last of the Mohicans

The theme of captivity shows up later in American fiction, as seen with James Fenimore Cooper's *The Last of the Mohicans* (1826).

Captivity narratives like Rowlandson's give us a firsthand account of the serious troubles settlers experienced in the seventeenth century. They reveal much about how Native Americans and English settlers were forever and irrevocably changed by their contact with each other, each driving to maintain a claim on the precious lands they each called home.

THE PURITANS

Godly Literature

What comes to mind when you think of the beginning of America? Probably the Pilgrims, right? (Or the Puritans ... wait, what's the difference?) The search for religious freedom? Or maybe that familiar glossy image of Native Americans and Pilgrims shaking hands over the first Thanksgiving table. All of these things are "true," but in what sense?

ONE IS NOT LIKE THE OTHER

The beginning of America is commonly associated with the English colonization of the North American continent, and an important element of that colonization was the Pilgrims and their search for freedom from religious persecution. It also begins with the venerable Pilgrim William Bradford's peaceful contract with the Native Americans. And it also begins with people who had other goals in mind—goals that had nothing to do with religion. Indeed, not all of the passengers on the *Mayflower* were Puritans; some were out for more ... worldly interests. Some were out for greater economic and social mobility; some were out for a sense of exploration or for just plain fun, a rabble-rousing adventure.

The English colonization of America began with the establishment of three main colonies: that of Jamestown in 1607 led by Captain John Smith; that of Plymouth Colony in 1620 led by William Bradford; and that of the Massachusetts Bay Colony in 1630 led by John Winthrop. There are likely many reasons why Bradford's

Plymouth Colony stands out most in the American imagination, not least of which is the main ideal on which it was founded: live and let live alone. This is one of the cornerstones, the bread and butter, shall we say, of the American ideal.

JOHN SMITH'S JAMESTOWN

But let's start with the first to be established: the Jamestown settlement. In May 1607 a group of English people began the first permanent English settlement on the mainland of North America in what is now called Virginia. These colonists were looking for freedom— freedom to practice their religion, but mostly economic freedom. They felt stifled by the economic and social systems back home and wanted to break free of them.

The Jamestown settlement had a rough start. Famine, disease, and hostile relations with neighboring tribes constantly threatened the colony's survival. When a swashbuckling captain named John Smith gained control of the colony as governor, he helped to stabilize the colony by establishing friendly trade relations with the Powhatan tribes. This trade agreement helped the colonists survive its early years and serves as another symbol of one of the cornerstones of the American ideal: the freedom to pursue economic freedom.

You've heard of Pocahontas, right? Well, it was Captain John Smith's life that Pocahontas supposedly saved by throwing her body over his when her father, Chief Powhatan, was about to have him killed, according to John Smith himself, that is. (Smith was known to embellish stories, and no one knows the exact truth of the story.) Indeed, John Smith's *A Description of New England*, with its descriptions of the natural world and chronicles of the relationships between the Powhatan tribe and colonists, gives a lively, imaginative, first-person explorer's account of this early founding of America.

Now for the other two colonies: Massachusetts Bay Colony and Plymouth Colony. These two colonies were both founded on Puritan ideals, but there are key differences between their stories.

JOHN WINTHROP'S (REGAL) MASSACHUSETTS BAY COLONY

The Massachusetts Bay Colony was established in 1630 by John Winthrop in what is now called Massachusetts. Like the Jamestown colonists, Winthrop was driven to the New World by economic dissatisfaction in England, but he was mostly compelled by anti-Puritan policies. Winthrop was on a quest to find both economic and religious freedom.

Winthrop's brand of Puritanism emphasized the "elective" quality of Puritanism, according to which Puritans were an elect few chosen by God to lead by example. Winthrop and his group were *dissenters* but not *separatists*—that is, they did not want to separate from the Church of England. They wanted to "purify" the church back home by their shining example. In his famous sermon, "A Model of Christian Charity" Winthrop wrote that their colony was ordained by God to become a "city upon a hill" upon which the eyes of others would gaze and be inspired. It was very important to Winthrop that the eyes of the world were watching:

> If we shall deal falsely with our God in this work we have undertaken and so cause Him to withdraw His present help from us, we shall be made a story and a byword throughout the world. We

shall open the mouths of enemies to speak evil of the ways of God and all professors for God's sake; we shall shame the faces of many of God's worthy servants and cause their prayers to be turned into curses upon us, till we be consumed out of the good land whither we are going.

Indeed, Winthrop carefully wove an orderly and tightly knit system by which his colony would live, and it worked: He was elected governor twelve times!

WILLIAM BRADFORD'S PILGRIM COLONY

Some fifty miles south, William Bradford had his own Puritan colony at New Plymouth. Bradford established his colony in 1620 after the ship he and his fellow Puritans were traveling on (bet you can name the ship!) blew off course and landed at Plymouth Rock. His colony was made up of what we commonly know as the Pilgrims (you know, with the tall black hats and buckled shoes). Unlike Winthrop's colony, Bradford and his fellow Puritans wanted complete religious freedom for themselves. They did not see any use in reforming the Church of England, and simply wanted to be free of it: They were dissenters *and* separatists.

Bradford wrote histories of his colony, and in one we see how Bradford read into everyday actions signs of God's "election." When one person was behaving uncharitably and died suddenly, Bradford read his death as a sign from God that such behavior is not rewarded.

Two Leaders, Two Styles

Notably, Winthrop's colony suffered more internal squabbles than Bradford's. The more Winthrop tried to enforce different rules, the more fractured the colony became. Bradford's colony was more stable and established one of the first peace contracts with the Native Americans, one that lasted more than fifty years.

So there you have it: No two leadership styles were the same under the Puritan umbrella, and no two Puritan groups were exactly the same. Leadership styles, goals, and ways of structuring governments were different. This can be seen reflected even in the forms of literature each leader is remembered for: John Smith's *The Generall Historie of Virginia* reads like an explorer's account; William Bradford's *Of Plymouth Plantation* reads from the vantage point of a calm, collected history of his Plymouth colony; and John Winthrop's sermon "A Model of Christian Charity" is a sterling rhetorical example meant to persuade readers of the merits of Puritan principles and his colony's efforts.

The Low-Down on Puritanism

Puritans held these core beliefs:

- The Church of England should be "purified" of Roman Catholic influence; no pope or bishop should interfere with a Christian soul's relationship to God;
- God has already chosen those he would save and those he would damn (doctrine of election); most of us are already depraved when born;
- Christ made an agreement with God to save all those who believed in him with his crucifixion (covenant of grace).

EARLY AMERICAN POETRY

Frontier Voices

The first published American poets represented the average colonist's concerns with religion and pioneer life, and their poetry explored themes of worship, Christian doctrine, and the hardships of being a pioneer in the New World. Anne Bradstreet, Edward Taylor, and Phillis Wheatley are three important poets whose poetry gives us a glimpse into these themes that shaped early American life.

ANNE BRADSTREET

Anne Bradstreet (1612–1672) is America's first published poet, and on top of that, she's also America's first published *female* poet. She began writing poetry as a young girl to please her father and picked up the craft again once she became a wife and settler in the New World, using it as a vehicle to express her wildly new experiences.

Bradstreet was a member of John Winthrop's Massachusetts Bay Colony, the group of Puritans who were not separatists but who hoped to renew England with their example of Puritan values of dignity, grace, and divine mission in the New World.

Bradstreet came from a privileged family in England and enjoyed all of the advantages of a wealthy upbringing, including a top-notch education not available to most women at the time. When Bradstreet set foot in North America for the first time, however, she found a "new world and new manners" in front of her, which sharply contrasted with the comfortable life she had back home. Her easy life of singing and entertaining was now replaced with hard labor and a near-constant threat of starvation.

Loving Wife

One of Bradstreet's most famous poems is "To My Dear and Loving Husband." It begins, "If ever two were one, then surely we. / If ever man were loved by wife, then thee." She wrote it about her husband, Simon Bradstreet, to whom she was married for forty-four years.

Some Puritans bemoaned their new situation (some even wished to drown in the Atlantic rather than face the enormous struggle of frontier life), but for Bradstreet, it strengthened her faith in the existence of God and her Puritan beliefs. Being so close to God's "wondrous works" day in and day out proved to Bradstreet that God existed and convinced her that the Puritan experiment in America was right. Bradstreet reflected these beliefs throughout her poetry.

Bradstreet's Poetic Themes

Bradstreet's poems tell of her love for her husband, notable events in her life such as losing her home to a fire, and meditations on life. In her poem "A Dialogue Between Old England and New," Bradstreet imagines a dialogue between "Old England" and "New England," where "New England" assures "Old England" (perhaps smugly) that her sufferings are not in vain, and that the Puritans' breach of allegiance to her will prove to renew England in all its spiritual purity. "New England" tells "Old England" to "cease complaints, and wipe your eyes," and that "Old England" will have to "tell another tale" once she bears witness to the success and glory of the Puritan experiment.

EDWARD TAYLOR (1642–1729)

While Bradstreet was in America writing her landmark poetry, back in England, another Puritan was also writing poetry to glorify the grace of God and was getting ready to set sail to America to become another member of the Puritan experiment. Not much is known about Edward Taylor's early life. His grandson, Ezra Stiles, who later became president of Yale University, described him as "A man of small stature, but firm; of quick Passions, yet serious and grave." Taylor's poetry was bequeathed to the Yale University Library in 1883, but it wasn't until 1939 that they were published and people had a chance to discover and read his vast body of work. His poems were private meditations on church doctrine, and often used as a way for him to work out ideas in his sermons. Taylor was a sought-after minister, known for his keen intellect.

Huswifery

Huswifery means "housekeeping." In early New England, a housewife's activities including spinning wool for clothing. Taylor uses this activity as a metaphor in his poem.

We do know Taylor grew up on a farm in England and had a relatively quiet life as a yeoman's son. In his poetry, Taylor often used the imagery of farming and the dialect he experienced in his early life. In his poem "Huswifery," for example, he uses the metaphor of weaving to describe a holy desire to be of service to God:

Make me, O Lord, Thy spinning-wheel complete.
Thy holy word my distaff make for me.
Make mine affections Thy swift flyers neat
And make my soul Thy holy spool to be.
My conversation make to be Thy reel
And reel the yarn thereon spun of Thy wheel.

Taylor's use of weaving in this poem is an example of a conceit, a special kind of metaphor. A *conceit* is an extended metaphor that compares two unlikely subjects over the course of a poem—in this case, the craft of spinning and weaving and the poet's body. Conceits were popular with the metaphysical poets of the seventeenth century, a group of poets whose poems often used conceits to work out complicated religious arguments while expressing joy and devotion to God. Their poems were unique in that they combined passion with abstract thought in highly intellectual ways. Taylor was especially influenced by one metaphysical poet in particular, George Herbert. Herbert's inventive uses of poetry were influential in his time. In his poem "Easter Wings," Herbert wrote his poem in the shape of wings across the page.

Metaphor and Simile

This is probably a good place to explain the difference between a metaphor and a simile. Metaphors and similes are literary devices poets and writers use to give life to a subject. A *metaphor* is a literary device that compares two things. For example, in the poem "In a Station of the Metro" by Ezra Pound, people's faces are compared to flower petals:

The apparition of these faces in the crowd;
Petals on a wet, black bough.

A *simile*, on the other hand, is a literary device that also compares two things, but uses the words "like" or "as." The poet Robert Frost uses a simile in his poem "Birches" to compare birch trees and girls:

> You may see their trunks arching in the woods
> Years afterwards, trailing their leaves on the ground
> Like girls on hands and knees that throw their hair
> Before them over their heads to dry in the sun.

Now isn't that a lot better than just saying that "sometimes people's faces in a crowd seem really white" or "birches bend their trunks in the woods"?

PHILLIS WHEATLEY (C. 1753–1784)

In 1761, a wealthy tailor named John Wheatley purchased a young female black slave for his wife as a companion. Though the young girl was weak in health, she showed signs of high intelligence. They named the young girl Phillis after the ship that carried her to Boston from her native Senegal in Africa. Unlike most slave owners of the time, the Wheatley family gave the young girl an education. Little did they know that this young girl would eventually make history.

Phillis was, in fact, a child prodigy. She began writing poetry and published her first poem at age thirteen. The poem, "On the Death of the Rev. Mr. George Whitefield, 1770," shows a young poet of great lyrical skill:

> But, though arrested by the hand of death,
> Whitefield no more exerts his laboring breath,
> Yet let us view him in the eternal skies,

Let every heart to this bright vision rise;
While the tomb safe retains its sacred trust,
Till life divine re-animates his dust.

Wheatley's owners encouraged her literary pursuits, and with their support, she went on to produce her first book of poetry, *Poems on Various Subjects, Religious and Moral*, in 1773. Aware that the book would cause a stir, the publishers arranged for a special preface to the book in which seventeen men of notable reputation testified that Phillis Wheatley was truly its author.

Biblical Symbolism

Wheatley often used biblical symbolism in her poetry to comment on slavery, which can be seen prominently in her most famous poem, "On Being Brought from Africa to America."

At a time when most women did not have access to an education, it was inconceivable that a woman, let alone a black slave, would write a book of poetry. With the publication of the book, Wheatley became both the first African American, and the first African-American woman, to publish a book of poetry.

THE ENLIGHTENMENT

The Rise of Reason

Within seventy-five years of the Puritans' first footsteps on the Eastern Seaboard, deep cracks were already showing in the beliefs that formed the basis of their carefully woven, deeply pious societies. More and more, Puritans bickered and split hairs over traditional rituals such as taking communion and central ideas like the doctrine of election. Communities began to splinter as groups began to take sides and stake new claims as to what it meant to be Puritan.

Back in England, however, an even greater threat to Puritan doctrine was beginning to emerge: An outbreak of new scientific and mathematical discoveries had begun to take hold and was about to break up the political, scientific, and religious frameworks that dominated Europe and the new colonies. These ideas are part of what we now refer to as the Age of Reason, or the Enlightenment.

NEWTON AND LOCKE

The Enlightenment owes its beginning to the work of two figures: Sir Isaac Newton (1642–1727) and John Locke (1632–1704). Their mathematical and scientific discoveries and philosophical works were so profound that they gave birth to an entire new world of philosophy that eventually turned the Puritan worldview on its head and laid the groundwork for two giant political revolutions in the eighteenth century: the American Revolution and French Revolution.

Pretty huge, right? Well, Newton and Locke didn't exactly intend to set off such a time bomb, or at least not in the Puritans' backyard.

Locke was raised by Puritan parents and didn't see a conflict between the ideas in his landmark publication *An Essay Concerning Human Understanding* (1690) and Christian doctrine.

Tabula Rasa and the Power of Reason

Formally, Locke's essay was a refutation on the philosophical notion of *innate ideas,* or the idea that humans are born with ideas and knowledge already inside of them. He argued instead that each human is born as a *tabula rasa,* or a "blank slate" onto which ideas and knowledge gained from experience and the senses are written. Accumulations of observations and sensations gained through our five senses, as well as our perceptions, eventually form new knowledge and ideas in us.

As with Locke, when Newton published his *Principia Mathematica* (1687) he wasn't setting out to refute Christian doctrine; he was laying the foundational groundwork of the laws of the universe. But between Locke's philosophical arguments and Newton's new scientific discoveries and frameworks, a new way of looking at the world was born. Nature was now seen as an orderly system, knowable through the faculty of reason. Through our own reason alone we could understand its laws—no God needed.

Nature's Laws

So let's break that down. *Humans could understand nature's laws by reason alone.* What does that mean? To us now, this may seem obvious. We know that we can discover the laws of nature using our minds and that these "laws" nature operates by are the ones that scientists use to ground their discoveries (and test and refute, test and refute, etc. their discoveries).

God Is No Longer Lurking . . .

But this wasn't how the average seventeenth-century individual thought of the universe, and certainly not the Puritans. The universe was largely understood as being *operated by the hand of God*. The things that happened to you on a daily basis were interpreted as signs of God's benevolent (or punishing) hand. Why did that apple fall (in front of you, and almost on your head)? Well, it must be God trying to send you a message. Maybe you are being warned—you've been telling too many white lies to your spouse and—lest you forget!—God is noticing. The occurrences of daily life were a sort of "revealed religion," which could and should be read emblematically and allegorically. God revealed himself to you in your life in these mysterious ways, and it was up to you and your clergyman to unlock the messages so that you could follow God's path.

As we all know, to Newton that apple fell for another reason: gravity. With Newton's groundbreaking discovery of the law of gravity, the world became a more rational place. This opened up a new way of thinking where God no longer took center stage. The world was rationally comprehensible to us now, and its workings were no longer a product of revelations by God. It also seemed a friendlier place—God wasn't lurking behind you trying to teach you lessons. Locke's idea of the *tabula rasa* implied that we are not born depraved as the Puritans thought, but rather born with a fresh moral slate.

The revelations of the Enlightenment ended up having an enormous impact on every major branch of learning, and decidedly and dramatically shifted the course of the thinking of the time. Scientists, philosophers, politicians, and other thinkers were now largely interested in grappling with the meaning of our own human nature and its own faculties of reason rather than reading the world emblematically. Religious leaders and thinkers had to respond to these revelations as well. Deism and deists attempted to reconcile these new scientific discoveries with religion by reasoning that the existence of God is proven by the beauty of the laws of the universe, not the Bible.

"Dare to know! Have courage to use your own reason!"

The Enlightenment may have had its roots in England, but its ideas spread far and wide. The German philosopher Immanuel Kant wrote that appeal in his 1784 essay "Answering the Question: What Is Enlightenment?" and it is an oft-cited definition of the Enlightenment. Kant defines *enlightenment* as an act of courage by an individual who dares to use his or her intellect.

. . . But Locke Is

Naturally, this upheaval had an effect on the literature produced in Europe and in America. Public-facing devotional texts gave way to more private, impassioned diary entries and chronicles. Histories of societies such as William Bradford's eventually gave way to more rhetorically structured political essays. You could now hear Locke lurking behind sermons blasted from Puritan pulpits. The minds of the world were ablaze with the new light cast by the torches of Locke and Newton. People were daring to know their world, from the inside out.

JONATHAN EDWARDS

Fire and Brimstone Preacher

Imagine you are an eighteenth-century Puritan, sitting in the pews with your family. A formidable presence speaks to you from the pulpit. His voice is steady, calm, and booming. He explains how, just like the Israelites of the Bible, you too shall be punished and your life destroyed by an angry God if you let yourself sink into sin.

As he describes how your soul will turn "into a fiery oven, or a furnace of fire and brimstone" the moment you slip and how hell, into which you will inevitably be tossed, is a place where "arrows of death fly" and a "rotten covering" lies upon the ground, you start to hear the people around you breathe more heavily, clearly distressed. As he goes on, some people even start to weep. Finally, more parishioners cry out with fear—they can't take it anymore—"Save me!" they yell out. But the preacher continues on, voice still steady, sermon book in hand, delivering his piercing message.

You're All Sinners!

According to historians, this is what it was like when preacher Jonathan Edwards (1703–1758) delivered his famous sermon "Sinners in the Hands of an Angry God" on July 8, 1741, from a pulpit in Connecticut. Not too pleasant. Here's an excerpt:

This . . . is the case of every one of you that are out of Christ. That world of misery, that lake of burning brimstone, is extended abroad under you. There is the dreadful pit of the glowing flames of the wrath of God; there is hell's wide gaping mouth open; and you have nothing to stand upon, nor any thing to take hold of;

there is nothing between you and hell but the air; 'tis only the power and mere pleasure of God that holds you up.

BACK TO THE OLD WAYS

At the time Edwards delivered his speech, the Enlightenment was well underway. Locke's ideas had infiltrated the colonies, and as to be expected, there was a backlash. Some theologians wanted to restore the Puritan church back to the "old ways" in the face of these new ideas. Jonathan Edwards was one of these theologians.

Locke's Treasure

Edwards read Locke and referred to his works as a "treasure." Drawing from Locke's theory of the senses and experiential knowledge, he felt Locke confirmed his belief that it wasn't enough for his congregation to understand Christian doctrine and follow it diligently. They had to know the feelings of religious devotion experientially to know what was meant by God's grace.

Rush of God

Only through feeling the rush of God's love could one be genuinely moved toward salvation and out of one's natural depraved, sinful nature. As Edwards wrote in his sermon, the Israelites' dire fate taught us the lesson that:

Natural men's prudence and care to preserve their own lives, or the care of others to preserve them, don't secure 'em a moment. This divine providence and universal experience does also bear testimony to. There is this clear evidence that men's own wisdom is no security to them from death; that if it were otherwise we should see some difference between the wise and politick men of the world, and others, with regard to their liableness to early and unexpected death: but how is it in fact? Ecclesiastes 2:16: "How dieth the wise man? Even as the fool."

No amount of Bible study, church visits, and other "do-good-ing" could get you a free pass from God. You couldn't escape hell by acing your prayers and following doctrine to the letter. You had to be *moved* to salvation by a sense of ecstasy and delight that you *felt*, with the experience of God, and then you understood. Edwards stood firm in this belief.

Edwards was one of the most formidable minds in American history. He had big shoes to fill since his grandfather was once referred to as the "Pope of the Connecticut Valley" and held much influence over the area. Edwards was admitted to Yale at age thirteen and graduated a few years later. For most of his life, he studied thirteen hours a day, never wanting "to lose one moment of time, but to improve it in the most profitable way." Once he was established in his own right as a preacher, he spent the rest of his life trying to imbue his congregation with the feelings that originally impelled the Puritans to risk their lives sailing across an ocean and scratching out a life in the New World.

Chapter 2

Literature of a Growing Republic

Between 1750 and 1800, Americans made a revolutionary break from England. The writing produced during this time was much less personal and soul-searching than that of the early English settlers. By this point, the colonies were relatively stable and established, and people were intent on education and improving their lives.

Speeches, pamphlets, broadsides, proclamations, declarations—America was deluged by public writing during this time, clearly influenced by the revolutionary spirit. Even personal writing meant to record the life and times of major public figures and events, such as *The Autobiography of Benjamin Franklin*, had a public flavor to it. People knew they were in an exciting, volatile time that would go down in history.

Much of the literature of the revolutionary period was not only political but radical. Writers such as Thomas Paine created landmark works that drew on Enlightenment thinking to reach profound conclusions concerning the political systems in England and the colonies. Thomas Jefferson's Declaration of Independence became the language of radical independence, shaping the American consciousness and the American idea of freedom. Toward the end of this period, people began to yearn for a new literature to fit their new country.

THOMAS PAINE'S *COMMON SENSE*

A Call to the Common Man

Born a corset-maker's son in England, Thomas Paine (1737–1809) found himself at odds with the world into which he was born. At eight years old, while listening to a sermon, he perceived a cruel streak in Christianity that turned him from the religion for the rest of his life. Paine had a formidable intelligence, and his willingness to rely on his God-given faculty of reason made him a poster child for the Enlightenment. Eventually his rebellious intelligence led to his place in history as the most powerful rhetorician for American independence. Without Paine's talent for distilling complex arguments into lively, easy-to-understand rhetoric, the colonists might not have unified under the cause.

Adams on Paine

John Adams wrote in 1805: "I know not whether any man in the world has had more influence on its inhabitants or affairs for the last thirty years than Tom Paine."

Paine the Radical

Thomas Paine rallied against many causes: As an excise tax collector, he tried to unionize his fellow excisemen for better pay (an unprecedented move for the time); as a pamphleteer in Philadelphia, he became the most brilliant articulator of the American cause for revolution; as a spokesman for the French Revolution, he (surprisingly) found himself arguing against the execution of the king. Over the course of his life he found himself calling for three main things: the abolition of a heredity monarchy, the equality of rights for man, and the superiority of reason.

An Unlikely Friend

Paine didn't come to America until he was thirty-seven years old. Shortly after Paine's attempt to unionize the excisemen ended in ridicule, Benjamin Franklin took notice of him and paid for him to go to America. Franklin likely recognized himself in Paine for they both were committed to the Enlightenment ideal of bettering oneself.

Pamphlets and Broadsides

Pamphlets and broadsides were a popular way to communicate from the sixteenth to the eighteenth centuries, especially during times of civil unrest. They were a cheap, immediate, and efficient way to spread political ideas quickly. Pamphlets such as Paine's *Common Sense* were printed on both sides, folded, and had a simple binding. Broadsides were usually one sheet and printed on one side, like the modern-day flyer. A famous example is the Dunlap broadside published on July 4 and 5, 1776, by printer John Dunlap. It featured a copy of the newly adopted Declaration of Independence.

When Paine arrived in Philadelphia in 1774, the cause for independence was reaching a fever pitch. The Boston Tea Party had happened the year prior, and the Second Continental Congress would shortly form to discuss the question of independence at hand. Not everyone in the colonies was for independence; some were worried that the colonies could not survive without Britain, especially economically. Then came Paine's pamphlet, *Common Sense*, published in 1776. The pamphlet spread like wildfire and sold nearly half a million copies. It won the minds and hearts of the colonists over to the cause of independence.

Fighter for the Common Man

The success of Paine's pamphlet rested on a few key things: It simplified complex legal precedents so they were easy to understand; it used strong, clear language that appealed to people's emotions; and it used simple analogies to illustrate carefully structured arguments. Always a fighter for the common man, Paine crafted his pamphlets with "no ceremonious expressions" and in language "as plain as the alphabet" in order "to make those who can scarcely read understand" something as complex as the nature of politics. Paine's writing approach reflected the Enlightenment (and Democratic) idea that, to understand politics, all it takes is common sense.

Rhetoric

The word *rhetoric* comes from the root word *rhetor* meaning "speaker" or "orator" and refers to speech and writing with the goal of persuasion. The art of rhetoric has a long history, the definition of which was formally established by Aristotle in his treatise *Rhetoric*. Aristotle says a rhetorician has three means by which to persuade his audience: his credibility, the emotions of his audience, and his logic. Thomas Paine's *Common Sense* skillfully blends all three.

For every argument uncertain colonists might have against independence, Paine had a carefully reasoned counterargument, which he clarified with simple analogies. For those colonists who were worried they would no longer flourish without Britain's help, he reasoned that as long as "eating is the custom of Europe," there would be trade outlets for the American states. Using the vivid analogy of a parent to a child (a common metaphor for Britain's relation to the colonies), he wrote that "we may as well assert that because a child has thrived upon milk, that it is never to have meat, or that the first twenty years of our lives is to become a precedent for the next twenty."

Paine went on to produce three other landmark works: *The American Crisis, Rights of Man*, and *The Age of Reason*. *The American Crisis* was so inspiring that George Washington had it read to his soldiers before crossing the Delaware River.

Eventually Paine lost favor in America because of his rough personality and went back to England where he wrote *Rights of Man,* which was a key argument against the heredity monarchy and for the equality of rights and land reform. After this, he wrote *The Age of Reason,* a continuation of Locke's idea that reason alone can be the source of the revelation of God. People felt he went too far in his denunciation of Christianity, and he was ridiculed and ostracized by almost everyone.

"These are the times that try men's souls"

Paine was one to turn a phrase. *The American Crisis* opened: "These are the times that try men's souls. The summer soldier and the sunshine patriot will, in this crisis, shrink from the service of their country; but he that stands by it now, deserves the love and thanks of man and woman."

Paine often found himself on the unpopular side of opinion, being ridiculed, thrown out of jobs, and exiled from countries. In perhaps the biggest irony, he died a despised man in the country he had a large hand in establishing—America.

THOMAS JEFFERSON

Author of the Declaration of Independence

In Thomas Jefferson's *Autobiography*, Jefferson (1743–1826) gives his firsthand account of the events surrounding the Declaration of Independence. He writes how Congress felt under the gun to produce a written declaration of independence from Britain, even as a few colonies were still dragging their feet:

> It appearing in the course of these debates, that the colonies of New York, New Jersey, Pennsylvania, Delaware, Maryland, and South Carolina were not yet matured for falling from the parent stem, but that they were fast advancing to that state, it was thought most prudent to wait a while for them, and to postpone the decision to July 1st; but, that this might occasion a little delay as possible, a committee was appointed to prepare a Declaration of Independence.

The committee formed to write and produce the Declaration of Independence consisted of John Adams, Benjamin Franklin, Roger Sherman, Robert Livingston, and Jefferson. And so the committee to prepare the Declaration of Independence—*the* keystone document of America's independence from Britain—began!

COMMANDING FIGURE

Jefferson's grandson described his grandfather as having a "commanding" stature, "robust health," and a "naturally strong" temper.

It was Jefferson's firm belief that the colonies should declare independence, and his bold and courageous temperament often carried over into his language. Jefferson's writing style was clear, direct, and forceful. He used highly charged words like *tyranny*, *infidel*, *honor*, and *liberty* in his writing to describe the colonists' desire to break free from Britain. His strong language shaped the idea of what independence meant for the colonists in the eighteenth century.

A Political Writer

In 1774, two years before drafting the Declaration of Independence, Jefferson wrote a pamphlet titled *A Summary View of the Rights of British America*, which declared that any authority Britain had over America was voluntary and could be revoked at any time by the colonists. This was a bold statement. The highly influential pamphlet established Jefferson as a radical but also as a skillful political writer. It was part of the reason why Congress sought him to write the Declaration of Independence.

Jefferson drafted the Declaration of Independence in less than three weeks—from June 11, 1776, to June 28, 1776. He records in his *Autobiography* that the "Committee for drawing the Declaration of Independence, desired me to do it," and he "reported it to the House on Friday, the 28th of June, when it was read, and ordered to lie on the table." The Congress returned to the document, which had lain on the table for the weekend, and debated it for the next three days—July 1, 2, and 3. With a few revisions, they finally adopted the declaration on July 4, 1776.

A Record of History in the Making

As a record of Congress's debate, Jefferson published the original draft of the Declaration of Independence in his *Autobiography* in

AMERICAN LIT 101

its entirety, including explanations for the revisions. In the original version, he underlined parts that Congress either struck from the document or revised, adding the revised text in the margins.

Parallel Structure

Parallel structure is a grammatical term referring to the use of phrases, clauses, and sentences that are similar in structure. For instance, consider the lines:

> We hold these truths to be self-evident, that all men are created equal, that they are endowed by their Creator with certain unalienable rights, that among these are life, liberty, and the pursuit of happiness.

Notice how each clause begins with the word *that.* Many Enlightenment writers favored parallel structure to give their writing the clarity and elegance that reflected rational thought. It's also why Jefferson's lines here are so memorable. (Give it a try—find more examples of parallel structure in the Declaration of Independence!)

Many of the revisions show how Congress tried to soften the blows of Jefferson's more forceful and incendiary language. Bold and unequivocal statements like "these states reject and renounce all allegiance to the kings of Great Britain" were stricken from the document and replaced with softer statements: "these united colonies are, and of right ought to be free and independent states." The revisions show a desire by Congress to make the document seem less defiant and to let the power of the document's statement rest on the strength of its argument rather than raw, courageous, and emotional declarations.

Congress deleted two major passages from Jefferson's original draft that reveals two main concerns Congress grappled with: that the institution of slavery should continue to exist, and that friendly relations with the British people should be maintained. One deleted passage criticized Britain for engaging in slavery, calling it "an execrable commerce"; another censured the British people for idly standing by a corrupt king. Jefferson noted these changes and the reasons behind Congress's decision to make them, but didn't state whether he was ultimately happy with these revisions or not. By publishing the original passages, however, Jefferson made clear that he wanted it publicly documented that he thought it was the *British people's complacency* that led to the revolution.

A "Pusillanimous Idea"

Jefferson *did* make it clear in no uncertain terms that he thought anything short of openly renouncing the British people forever was cowardly. In explaining why Congress took out the passage criticizing the British, he wrote "the pusillanimous idea that we had friends in England worth keeping terms with, still haunted the minds of many." (*Pusillanimous* means "cowardly, fearful.")

NICE GUY

When the first Library of Congress was burned by the British during the War of 1812, Jefferson sold his personal library of about 6,500 volumes to Congress. The collection became the foundation for the collections of the Library of Congress in Washington, D.C., that exists today. When Jefferson was seventy-six, he founded the University of Virginia, to which he left most of his library when he died in 1826.

I Wrote It

Jefferson went on to achieve many more remarkable things: He became the first secretary of state under George Washington, became vice president in 1796, and was the first president to be inaugurated in Washington in 1800. In his leisure time he was an accomplished architect, gardener, scientist, and inventor. But of all these things, Jefferson made it clear that he wanted to be remembered for writing the Declaration of Independence.

THE WRITINGS OF BENJAMIN FRANKLIN

American Wisdom

Benjamin Franklin (1706–1790)—printer, writer, publisher, statesman, inventor, postmaster, diplomat, Founding Father. Quite the list, right? Franklin was one of the most important individuals in American history. He was elected to the Second Continental Congress, became a diplomat to both Britain and France, and was a member of the Constitutional Convention. He served in many public offices, and his inventions like the bifocal lens, the Franklin stove, and the lightning rod aimed to improve the quality of life. He was a true public servant. He was also one of America's finest writers.

Ladies' Man

Benjamin Franklin: printer, writer, publisher, statesman, inventor, diplomat, and . . . ladies' man? Yup, Franklin earned quite the reputation with women. Letters, drawings, and other evidence prove Franklin was an undeniable flirt, and enjoyed sparring with intellectual women.

A FATHER'S GUIDING HAND

As a Founding Father, Franklin had a hand in writing four key documents: the Declaration of Independence (1776); the Treaty of Alliance with France (1778); the Treaty of Paris, which ended the

Revolutionary War (1783); and the U.S. Constitution (1787), which formally established the United States.

Franklin began his career as a printer at age twelve. He didn't want to take up his father's candle-making business, and his older brother James was already a printer, so Franklin's father decided to make a printer out of his younger son as well. Franklin didn't like the printing business and threatened to run away to sea, but that never happened. He did, however, run away to Philadelphia at age seventeen to live on his own. He famously showed up with a few coins in his pocket and nothing else.

Franklin's *Autobiography*

All of this is documented in *The Autobiography of Benjamin Franklin*, one of the finest autobiographies in literary history. Franklin began writing the book late in life for his son William, who was a British loyalist and the last colonial governor of New Jersey. The language is clear, direct, and elegant. Franklin had a forceful style, using strong verbs and vivid details. In the work, he traces the stepping stones on the path to becoming the man he was.

In Chapter II, Franklin describes how he came across the Socratic method as a young man, a style of arguing that was less fiery than his natural manner. His method of remaining aloofly engaged in conversation became a trademark of his public persona and contributed to his great success as a diplomat:

> While I was intent on improving my Language, I met with an English Grammar (I think it was Greenwood's) at the End of which there were two little Sketches of the Arts of Rhetoric and Logic, the latter finishing with a Specimen of a Dispute in the Socratic Method. And soon after I procur'd Xenophon's *Memorable Things of Socrates*, wherein there are many Instances of

the same Method. I was charm'd with it, adopted it, dropped my abrupt Contradiction and positive Argumentation, and put on the humble Enquirer and Doubter...I took Delight in it, practic'd it continually and grew very artful and expert in drawing People even of superior Knowledge into Concessions, the Consequences of which they did not forsee, entangling them in Difficulties out of which they could not extricate themselves, and so obtaining Victories that neither myself nor my Cause always deserved.

In Chapter IX, he goes into great detail about how he decided to embark on the "arduous Project of arriving at moral Perfection," saying he "wish'd to live without committing any Fault at anytime." After analyzing the reasons why, despite the best intentions, he slipped back into bad habits, he deduced that "Habit took the Advantage of Inattention" and set about correcting his bad habits one at a time.

FRANKLIN'S *POOR RICHARD'S ALMANACK*

Franklin thought long and hard about the different virtues preached during his time and reduced them to a neat and tidy list of thirteen he would try to master: temperance, silence, order, resolution, frugality, industry, sincerity, justice, moderation, cleanliness, tranquility, chastity, and humility. He even created charts of his progress toward each virtue, marking the charts with a dot if he failed one day!

When Franklin became the owner of a printing business he decided to share his hard-earned knowledge and published a book of advice on the ways to wealth, health, and wisdom in a series called

Poor Richard's Almanack. The series was a success and made Franklin wealthy. It contains all the maxims we most know Franklin for, such as, "Early to bed, early to rise, makes a man healthy, wealthy and wise" and "There are no gains without pains." (*Maxims* are short sayings that express truths about ways to live.)

Not a Fan

Benjamin Franklin may be one of the most beloved figures in American history, but not everyone was a fan. Mark Twain wrote a sniping essay, "The Late Benjamin Franklin," about Franklin in his *Essays and Sketches of Mark Twain.* Soured by Franklin's influence over the American mind, Twain wrote that he "desired to do away with somewhat of the prevalent calamitous ideas among heads of families that Franklin acquired his great genius by working for nothing, studying by moonlight, and getting up in the middle of the night instead of waiting till morning like a Christian; and that this program, rigidly inflicted, will make a Franklin of every father's fool." Rather, Twain argued, these "execrable eccentricities of instinct and conduct are only the *evidences* of genius, not the *creators* of it." Twain had a bone to pick with Franklin because his parents had tried to "make him a Franklin" by forcing him to go to bed early as a boy.

Franklin's long and influential life made him a paragon for the American ideal of making it on one's own. He grew up poor, but through hard work, persistence, and dedication, he achieved a life of wealth, learning, and prestige.

JOHN AND ABIGAIL ADAMS

Love Letters to America

John Adams (1735–1826) had a glorious career as one of America's Founding Fathers. He served as a member of the First and Second Continental Congresses, helped to draft the Declaration of Independence, served on several diplomatic missions to Europe alongside Ben Franklin, and became the second president of the United States in 1796. His astute political sense and innovative political solutions played a key role in the shaping of the nation. And who was one of his chief advisors in the background? His wife, Abigail.

Abigail Adams was born in 1744 in Weymouth, Massachusetts. Her father was a beloved and highly esteemed Congregationalist minister. She had no formal schooling, but she was extremely intelligent and had a keen appetite for learning. She read anything she could find: the Bible, books on philosophy, political essays, poetry, and histories. At age seventeen, she met John Adams, who lived in neighboring Braintree. They began exchanging love letters and married a few years later.

Continental Congresses

The Continental Congresses were conventions of delegates from the thirteen colonies formed to address tensions with Britain. The First Continental Congress met in 1774 after Britain punished the Massachusetts colonists for the Boston Tea Party by stripping them of certain rights. The Second Continental Congress met in the summer of 1775, after tensions between Britain and the colonists reached a fever pitch and the first acts of warfare occurred at Lexington and Concord in Massachusetts. The Second Continental Congress adopted the Declaration of Independence on July 4, 1776.

John Adams graduated from Harvard College in 1755 and after a short stint as a teacher began studying law. He was content to keep a law practice and a farm in Braintree, but found that he was better equipped to provide for his family if he lived in Boston.

In Boston, John found himself in the hotbed of politics. His public opposition to the Stamp Act of 1765 garnered him a reputation as a revolutionary, and he was called to serve as a member of the First Continental Congress. John Adams reported to duty in Philadelphia in June 1774, leaving Abigail and his family behind for ten years.

Over the years John was gone, John and Abigail wrote more than 300 letters to each other.

May We Snoop?

The letters of John and Abigail Adams, though very personal, have become a widely read and well-documented piece of revolutionary history. They provide a fascinating behind-the-scenes look into the opinions, attitudes, and beliefs that shaped the delegation's final decision to declare independence.

John's Opinion of Franklin: He's a Great Guy

In a letter to Abigail in July 1775, John answers his wife's request for more information about "Dr. Franklin." John replies with a letter that reveals not only his opinion of Franklin, but Franklin's unique role in the debates among the delegates:

Dr. Franklin has been very constant in his Attendance on Congress from the Beginning. His Conduct has been composed and grave and in the Opinion of many Gentlemen very reserved. He has not assumed any Thing, nor affected to take the lead; but has seemed to choose that Congress should pursue their

own Principles and sentiments and adopt their own Plans. . . .
He thinks, that We have the Power of preserving ourselves, and
that even if We should be driven to the disagreeable Necessity of
assuming a total Independency, and set up a separate state, We
could maintain it . . .

Adams had a great opinion of Franklin, writing, "I wish his Colleagues from this City were All like him."

Abigail the Political Advisor

Once it became clear that the colonies were heading for independence, Abigail was quick to give her opinions. She posed some hard
questions to John in a letter dated November 27, 1775:

I am more and more convinced that Man is a dangerous creature,
and that power whether vested in many or a few is ever grasping,
and like the grave cries give, give. The great fish swallow up the
small, and he who is most strenuous for the Rights of the people,
when vested with power, is as eager after the prerogatives of
Government. . . . The Building up a Great Empire, which was only
hinted at by my correspondent may now I suppose be realized
even by the unbelievers. Yet will not ten thousand Difficulties
arise in the formation of it? The Reigns of Government have been
so long slakned, that I fear the people will not quietly submit to
those restraints which are necessary for peace, and security, of
the community; if we seperate from Brittain, what Code of Laws
will be established. How shall we be governd so as to retain our
Liberties? Can any government be free which is not adminstred
by general stated Laws?

These were the same hard questions that the delegates would grapple with over the following years. Abigail's voice was in the back of John's mind as he sat at the table with his colleagues mapping out the fate of the nation.

Remember the Ladies

In one of the most famous letters Abigail wrote, dated March 31, 1776, she urged her husband and his fellow delegates to "Remember the Ladies" as they set out to define the nation's independence from Great Britain:

Remember the Ladies, and be more generous and favorable to them than your ancestors. Do not put such unlimited power into the hands of Husbands. Remember all Men would be tyrants if they could. If particular care and attention is not paid to the Ladies we are determined to foment a Rebellion, and will not hold ourselves bound by any Laws in which we have no voice, or Representation.

Abigail's warning was right: Almost a hundred years later, in Seneca Falls, New York, activists including Elizabeth Cady Stanton convened to "foment a Rebellion" on behalf of women in America to secure their right to vote.

PHILIP FRENEAU

The Poet of the American Revolution

While pamphlets, broadsides, speeches, and proclamations dominated the American literary landscape during the late eighteenth century, American poetry was still thriving—albeit in the background. The Puritan poets had set the stage, becoming the first published poets in the New World, but their subject matter was English. The colonists were beginning to yearn for their own, "American" literature that expressed the new America that was beginning to form. As the colonists broke free from Britain's rule, they were also eager to break free of its literature. It was time for a literature of America.

Ode

An ode is a lyric poem that celebrates, or commemorates, a person, place, thing, or idea. The form changed over the years as different ages adapted the form to its time and mood. During ancient Greek times, the poet Pindar (552–442 B.C.E.) wrote odes that were set to music and sung at public ceremonies. During the Latin era, the poet Horace (65 B.C.E.–C.E. 8) wrote odes that were less celebratory and more contemplative. In the eighteenth and nineteenth centuries, English romantic poets wrote odes that were more personal and captured internal struggles rather than public themes.

The writer Philip Freneau (1752–1832) tried to answer the call. Freneau came from a wealthy background and was a graduate of Princeton University. As a student at Princeton, he roomed with the future president James Madison. With another fellow student, Hugh

Henry Brackenridge, he cowrote an ode called "The Rising Glory of America," which was read at commencement. Not bad for a start in a literary career.

LOST AT SEA

It didn't take long, however, for Freneau to veer from this promising path. As a young man, he took a secretary position on a plantation far away in the West Indies. He developed an appreciation for nature and a sensuous lyrical style to capture the beauty of all the lush tropical vegetation of the island. Although the landscape certainly captured his imagination, after three years he grew tired of being a part of a slave economy and wanted to return home. It wasn't so easy: He was captured at sea by a British ship and imprisoned, suffering brutal treatment and abuse. This cemented in him a deep hatred of the British that lasted the rest of his life.

After many years at sea, Freneau found his way to Philadelphia where his college roommate James Madison tapped him to head the *National Gazette*, a newspaper that Madison and Thomas Jefferson founded. Jefferson and Madison hoped the newspaper would give voice to Anti-Federalist invectives against Alexander Hamilton and his Federalist policies. Freneau and his fellow Anti-Federalists found Hamilton's policies too conservative and dangerously close to monarchy.

"Poet of the American Revolution"

In Philadelphia, Freneau established his fame as a political writer. With his pen he explored many literary forms—newspaper articles, pamphlets, and, eventually, poems. With poems, Freneau set his sights on capturing the spirit of the revolution. He looked to none other than Thomas Paine as one of his first subjects.

Like Paine, Freneau developed a vicious grudge against the British systems; Freneau saw him as a heroic representative of the revolution. In one of his famous poems, "On Mr. Paine's *Rights of Man*," Freneau captures Paine's revolutionary spirit in one neat, heroic couplet:

> Thus briefly sketched the sacred rights of man,
> How inconsistent with the royal plan!

With poems like these, Freneau earned himself the title of "Poet of the American Revolution."

THROUGH "AMERICAN" EYES

But Freneau didn't stop there. As a poet gazing across the American landscape, he looked to other subjects that could be reimagined as "American." In his poem "The Indian Burying Ground," he celebrates the Indian, describing their custom of burying their dead seated rather than lying down:

> His bow, for action ready bent,
> And arrows, with a head of stone,
> Can only mean that life is spent,
> And not the old ideas gone.

In his poem "The Wild Honey Suckle," he glorifies the honeysuckle, a common flower in New England. He even took up the popular American tobacco plant as a theme.

An Older, Grumpier Freneau

As an older writer, Freneau now saw a new threat on the American landscape—newly successful American writers who were still looking backward to England. He was quick to mock those writers (in this case, Washington Irving) who were still flattering England and all its "glittering nobles" in his poem "To a New England Poet":

> See Irving gone to Britain's court
> To people of another sort,
> He will return, with wealth and fame,
> While Yankees hardly know your name.

A Swing and a Miss

Freneau may have been the "Poet of the American Revolution," but he can't be called the father of American poetry. While his themes were fresh and new, he was still writing in the English neoclassical tradition, which prioritized structure and formality, heroism, and old "classical" forms—all features Freneau heavily relied on. The push for American literature—in spirit and form—would continue long after Freneau.

Heroic Couplet

In the English neoclassical tradition, a popular poetic form was the heroic couplet. The heroic couplet is a tightly knit set of lines ending in rhyme. The English neoclassical poet Alexander Pope was considered the master of the heroic couplet. His poem "An Essay on Man" begins with a heroic couplet famous for capturing the spirit of the Enlightenment:

> Know then thyself, presume not God to scan;
> The proper study of mankind is man.

Paving the Way

Freneau may have missed the mark, but everyone agrees he was a giant in paving the way for later American writers. Some now see Freneau's "The Wild Honey Suckle" as a precursor to American transcendentalism, which also took native plants as a theme. In his gloomy poem "The House of Night," some see the glimmerings of the later American gothic writer Edgar Allan Poe.

WASHINGTON IRVING

Putting America on the Literary Map

After the revolution, America became the "birthplace of freedom" and a hub of sterling political and philosophical minds. But a cultural hub? Not so much. Americans may have broken the shackles of England politically, but they were still very much tied to England culturally, following England's tastes in fashion, literature, and music.

Ironically it was Washington Irving (1783–1859), a writer who lived most of his life in Europe, who raised American literature to international heights. Irving was born in New York City to a Scottish-born father and an English-born mother. As a young man he read widely and read many of the English greats such as Shakespeare, but he had a taste for adventure, not writing. He made attempts to run away to sea at age fourteen, but his parents, who named him after George Washington, had envisioned more illustrious heights for him. They forced him to study law instead.

Would the Real Mr. Irving Please Stand Up?

Irving adopted many pen names over his career: Geoffrey Crayon, Jonathan Oldstyle, Anthony Evergreen. For the publication of *A History of New York*, he created an elaborate ruse where he got the *New York Evening Post* to publish an article revealing the book was written and left behind by a mysterious man who was "not entirely of his right mind" named Diedrich Knickerbocker.

When Irving became ill in 1804 at the age of twenty-one, his family sent him to Europe to regain his health, and it was during this time he became a keen observer of the English. When he returned, he and his brother William started a magazine called *Salmagundi* (an English hodgepodge of meats, vegetables, nuts, and fruits), which was comprised of satirical reports and sketches of people in the New York scene. People lapped up this fresh, gossipy new voice in writing (although no one knew it was Irving—he wrote anonymously), but after a year the brothers got into a dispute with the publisher, and the magazine shut up shop.

Irving realized he had a flair for satire, and followed *Salmagundi* with *A History of New York*, a parody account of New York's history that combined fact with exaggeration and featured prominent New York figures with mock seriousness. No one was safe from his barbed pen; even Thomas Jefferson, who was president at the time, was spoofed. The book was hilarious and a huge success in its time and made Irving an international success—it was said that Charles Dickens carried it in his pocket. The fresh, irreverent style had an enormous impact on later American satirists such as Mark Twain.

Satire

A satire is a piece of writing that uses humor, exaggeration, and irony to expose or criticize people and society. A famous example of satire is Jonathan Swift's "A Modest Proposal," published in 1729, which mocked harsh British policies toward Ireland by suggesting the impoverished Irish sell their children to feed British's rich in order to pay back England.

Even with all of these successes, Irving had still yet to create the stories he is most known for: "Rip Van Winkle" and "The Legend of Sleepy Hollow." Irving included these stories in a serial collection called *The Sketch Book of Geoffrey Crayon, Gent.*, under the pen name Geoffrey Crayon. The series began when the English writer Sir Walter Scott, impressed by Irving's *A History of New York*, struck up a friendship with Irving and suggested to him a new source for his sketches: German folktales. Irving now enlarged his work by brilliantly setting his trademark realistic character sketches in authentic rural American settings woven against European traditions and fables with great results: Rip Van Winkle and the Headless Horseman are some of America's enduring and treasured characters.

Rip Van Winkle, Ben Franklin's Lazy Twin

So who are these characters? "Rip Van Winkle" was published in the last installment of *The Sketch Book* in 1819. Here Irving created an American "antihero," a laid-back figure who created success from ... not working. Rip is a beloved man of a small town near the Catskill Mountains. However, his wife continually nags him to get a job. He enjoys his leisure time, telling stories, giving presents, and going on solitary adventures in the Catskills. Rip decides to escape his wife's nagging by going to the woods and discovers a man dressed in Dutch clothing who asks him to help carry a keg. They walk up a mountain together and discover a group of men bowling. They offer Rip a drink and he falls asleep. When he wakes up, he learns that twenty years have passed and the American Revolutionary War has happened. Rip has slept through one of the most difficult periods in American history, unscathed. His story helped Americans have faith that, even if you didn't like to work hard, you might still become a success—on your own terms.

Sketch

A sketch is a short descriptive piece, usually written about something that is exotic and outside of the audience's culture. Sketches often had a characteristically informal, familiar style, as if the writer was "chatting" openly with the reader. Sketches were popular during Irving's time because they were a quick way to satisfy the public's curiosity about other places.

"The Legend of Sleepy Hollow"

Who doesn't have an image of the Headless Horseman tearing through a cemetery at night on a wild horse? Ichabod Crane, the enervated schoolteacher and his skinny horse, and Katrina Van Tassel, the rustic beauty and Crane's love interest, are characters who immediately captured readers' imaginations. The realistic depictions of the rural American landscape mixed with a tinge of the macabre influenced many writers after Irving. The story has been adapted many times since it was published, even forming the basis for a hit television series, *Sleepy Hollow*.

JAMES FENIMORE COOPER

Father of the American Novel

James Fenimore Cooper (1789–1851) began his literary career on a whim: While at home reading a British novel, he proudly announced to his wife that he could write a better one. His wife Susan challenged him to back it up, and he took the bet. Within a year he finished his first novel, *Precaution* (1820), about English high society. It was a flop.

Not one to give up (and supremely assured of his talent), Cooper persisted. He published another two novels in the next three years: *The Spy* in 1821 and *The Pioneers* in 1823. *The Spy* was one of the first historical romances of the American Revolution. With *The Pioneers*, he established himself as a worthy writer. The novel sold more than 3,500 copies and featured the character Cooper would become best known for: Natty Bumppo. Natty Bumppo was the first fictional American hero.

COOPER
THE REBELLIOUS PRANKSTER

As a young man, Cooper was a brilliant student, but he had a rebellious streak that often got him into trouble. While at Yale, he found gunpowder and used it to blow up a classmate's door. When he left a donkey in a classroom, university officials expelled him. Like many young males of his era, he was lured by the promise of adventure at sea and became a sailor. In 1809, he set sail on the British merchant ship the *Stirling*. While at sea, he experienced pirate attacks and drunken, insane sailors, and was targeted for impressment into the British Royal Navy. Eventually he settled down once he met the wealthy Susan De Lancey. When Cooper's father died, they moved to his enormous estate in New York.

Natty Bumppo, born to white parents, was also raised among the Delaware Indians and learned their skills. He was educated by Christians and so had a foot in both worlds. Adopted by the Mohicans Natty traveled alongside the Mohican chief, Chingachgook. Natty is physically strong, skilled, and knows how to survive in the wild. He becomes a frontier action hero, wise in the ways of both the frontier and the New World.

The Many Names of Natty

Natty Bumppo had many aliases. As a young man he earned the name Hawkeye for his ability to quickly spot deer. People called him Pathfinder because he found paths for many lost and helpless New Englanders through the woods. He earned the name Straight-Tongue for his honesty, and Deerslayer because of his skilled use of the long rifle. Finally, he earned the name Leatherstocking for the deerskin leggings he wore in his old age. In his Leatherstocking Tales, Cooper created several archetypes about American values and Native Americans that still survive today. Chingachgook represented the "noble red man," while Magua, a Huron chief in the novel *The Last of the Mohicans*, epitomized "the revengeful Indian." Natty Bumppo became synonymous with the American values of truth, honor, and masterful skill. The term "last of the Mohicans" came to mean the "last surviving noble man of a race" and referred to both the white man Natty and the Native American Chingachgook. The Leatherstocking Tales follow major stages in Natty's life. Cooper wrote them out of order, beginning with *The Pioneers*, which featured Natty as an old man.

YEAR PUBLISHED	BOOK TITLE	STAGE IN NATTY'S LIFE
1841	The Deerslayer	Natty as a young man, first coming to terms with his position as both a man of the frontier and a man of the New World
1826	The Last of the Mohicans	Natty at the height of his manhood and heroism; set during the French and Indian War
1840	The Pathfinder	A full-blown romance; Natty as middle-aged man, tempted to settle down in domestic bliss with a young woman (he doesn't)
1823	The Pioneers	Natty as an old man; a vanishing figure of nobility in the encroachment of civilization
1827	The Prairie	Natty in his last years; helping (regretfully inept) pioneers in the frontier

Mark Twain: A Writer's Worst Nightmare

Mark Twain was not someone to call to review your book if you were unsure it was up to snuff. Never shy of criticizing other's writing, Twain reviewed Cooper's work in a famous (and hilarious) essay called "Fenimore Cooper's Literary Offenses" in 1895. The following is a sampling of the "rules governing literary art" Twain cites Cooper for violating (Twain says Cooper violated at least 114 out of 115 of them in *The Deerslayer*):

- An overly wordy style: "Authors shall eschew surplusage"

- Unbelievable characterization: "When personages of a tale deal in conversation, the talk shall sound like human talk, and be talk such as human beings would be likely to talk in the given circumstances"
- Unreasonable plot lines: "Personages of a tale shall confine themselves to possibilities and let miracles alone"

Father of the American Novel

Cooper would go on to write five books about Natty, collectively called the Leatherstocking Tales. People over the world were enthralled with the Natty Bumppo character and the glimpse into the complexities of American life. The intricate, fast-paced, and exciting plotlines set against the exotic American frontier made the public hungry for more tales of Bumppo. With these books, James Fenimore Cooper firmly established himself as the "father of the American novel."

While Cooper's literary reputation grew to meteoric heights through his life, his personal reputation suffered. When critics attacked his writing in America and in England, he embroiled himself in countless lawsuits to counterattack the critics and protect his reputation. When people began picnicking on his vast property in New York, he sued them. He became known as a pretentious crank. By the end of his life his reputation was so bad that he requested his family to stop any account of his life from ever being published. Despite his problematic personality, Cooper's reputation as a renowned American writer still stands strong today.

Chapter 3

Creating an American Literature

By 1840, America had established itself politically, but its literature was still playing catch-up. Washington Irving and James Fenimore Cooper had elevated American literature in the world's eyes, captivating Europe with books set in the wild American landscape, but the nation didn't have a literature yet that defined its spirit. America thought it had its poet laureate in Henry Wadsworth Longfellow, the eminent professor at Harvard who created elegantly structured poems using traditional meters and forms to memorialize important figures in America's recent past, and Native Americans as well. But American literature was still a few decades off from finding its real poetic voice.

Shortly after 1840, America had a burst of creativity called the American Renaissance, during which a small group of writers produced some of the best and most creative writing in its literary history. The movement came on the heels of the romantic movement, which had swept across Europe in the late eighteenth and early nineteenth centuries and cleared the way for a more dramatic, imaginative, and instinctual literature. American writers now felt able to free themselves from old literary forms and traditions to produce creative work that came from their own impulses, whatever form those took.

And all the while writers were creating these works, the nation was approaching its next crisis—the Civil War. A crop of writers such as Harriet Beecher Stowe, Frederick Douglass, and Lydia Maria Child wrote works on the issue that would soon drive their country apart—slavery.

HENRY WADSWORTH LONGFELLOW

America's First Poet of Eminence

Pop quiz: Who wrote these famous lines?

> Listen, my children, and you shall hear
> Of the midnight ride of Paul Revere

The answer? Henry Wadsworth Longfellow (1807–1882), America's beloved poet of the nineteenth century and creator of some of the most enduring poems in American literature (including those lines from his poem "Paul Revere's Ride"). Longfellow gave America literary stature: In 1884, he became the first American poet to be honored in England when he was given a bust in the Poets' Corner of Westminster Abbey in London.

So who was this fellow, Longfellow? Henry Wadsworth Longfellow was born in Portland, Maine, in 1807. He came from a pretty high-profile background—his father was a well-educated lawyer, and his grandfather served as a general in the Revolutionary War. Longfellow attended Bowdoin College in Maine, where he met another future famous writer, Nathaniel Hawthorne, as well as other future important people. Longfellow's father wanted him to study law (of course), but in his senior year, Longfellow declared in a letter to his father: "I most eagerly aspire after future eminence in literature, my whole soul burns most ardently after it."

AN AMERICAN AESTHETE

During his time at Bowdoin, Longfellow particularly excelled at languages. When a professorship in language was created shortly after Longfellow graduated, the college offered him the post. The college sent Longfellow to Europe to further hone his language skills, deepen his knowledge of the literary traditions, and accustom him to the cultures of Europe—to essentially become an "aesthete" of European culture. Longfellow spent three years traveling across Europe, absorbing the customs, tastes, and arts of the major countries of Europe.

Quick Poetry Lesson

In poetry, lines are written with attention to *meter*, patterns of stressed and unstressed syllables. A unit of meter is called a *foot*. Poetry is written in a variety of meters—or ways of joining together feet. Poetic meter that joins together four trochees (a type of foot) in a line, for example, is called *trochaic tetrameter* (*tetra* means "four").

TYPES OF FEET	(STRESSED = S) (UNSTRESSED = U)	EXAMPLES (BOLD IS STRESSED)
Iamb	U/S	Shall **I** com**pare** thee **to** a **sum**mer's **day**?
Trochee	S/U	**Speak** in **tones** so **plain** and **child**like
Dactyl	S/U/U	**Loud** from its **ro**cky ca**verns**
Anapest	U/U/S	Listen, **my** children **and** you shall **hear**
Spondee	S/S	**With swift**, **slow**; **sweet**, **sour**; a**dazzle**, **dim**

While in Spain, Longfellow met and stayed for a time with another famous American writer, Washington Irving. Irving encouraged Longfellow to write his own sketchbook of observations of European life, like Irving's popular version. Longfellow started one called "The

Wondrous Tale of a Little Man in Gosling Green," published in the *New-Yorker* magazine (no relation to the famous *New Yorker* magazine of today, which started publishing in 1925) in 1834, but he lost interest and abandoned the project.

After his tour of Europe, Longfellow settled into his new country life: He assumed his professorship at Bowdoin, married a childhood friend, and had a comfortable existence. A bit too comfortable, though—Longfellow found his new life stifling compared to his cosmopolitan experiences abroad. Longfellow decided to move him and his wife to Cambridge, Massachusetts, where he took a new professorship post at Harvard College, a position he held for eighteen years.

Bringing Europe to America

At Harvard, Longfellow finally began to build the literary career he dreamed of. While building the modern language studies program at the college, he authored an anthology called *The Poets and Poetry of Europe*, which became a standard in literature courses. The anthology helped connect Americans to the vast literary traditions of Europe.

In essence, this was Longfellow's largest contribution to the world of letters: He brought Europe to America. He argued in his essay "Defence of Poetry" that "the true glory of a nation consists not in . . . the majesty of its rivers, the height of its mountains, and the beauty of its sky, but in the extent of its mental power—the majesty of its intellect—the height, and depth, and purity of its moral nature." Longfellow wanted to see American culture raised to the intellectual heights of Europe.

In his own writing, he put this into practice by domesticating European literary meters to use them on American subjects. Here are some famous examples.

"The Song of Hiawatha"

"The Song of Hiawatha" blended epic poetry and trochaic meter to tell the story of Hiawatha, an Ojibwe Indian. Longfellow modeled the meter of the poem on a Finnish epic poem called *The Kalevala*, which he read while abroad. Longfellow felt that the Finnish poem's trochaic tetrameter, a poetic meter that places the stress on the first syllable, best matched the rhythms of Native American speech. The effect is a very singsongy poetry:

> Ye who love a nation's legends,
> Love the ballads of a people,
> That like voices from afar off
> Call to us to pause and listen,
> Speak in tones so plain and childlike,
> Scarcely can the ear distinguish
> Whether they are sung or spoken;—
> Listen to this Indian Legend,
> To this Song of Hiawatha!

Can you hear the stress on the first syllable of each line? Poems like this were often viewed as examples of excellence in rhythm and meter. The poem was extremely popular and sold over 50,000 copies.

"Paul Revere's Ride"

"Paul Revere's Ride" was the first poem in Longfellow's popular collection of poetry, *Tales of a Wayside Inn*. In this collection, Longfellow modeled his poetry after the medieval English writer Geoffrey Chaucer's masterpiece, *The Canterbury Tales*. Longfellow used a narrative style and ballad form to immortalize important figures in his nation's recent history. "Paul Revere's Ride" was written in anapestic tetrameter, a meter he chose to match the rhythm of a galloping horse:

> Listen, my children and you shall hear
> Of the midnight ride of Paul Revere,
> On the eighteenth of April, in Seventy-Five:
> Hardly a man is now alive
> Who remembers that famous day and year.

Can you hear the galloping horse? This poem was also extremely popular in its time and arguably Longfellow's most remembered poem.

Out of Tune

Longfellow's poems were often used as examples in classrooms for recitation and memorization. Over the years, however, this singsong quality of poems like "The Song of Hiawatha" sounded childish to people's ears and was criticized for making a poem seem too sentimental.

Fireside Poets

Longfellow belonged to a group of poets called the Fireside Poets, a term used to describe the first group of American poets whose reputation was considered on par with that of the British masters. Other poets in this group included Oliver Wendell Holmes Sr., James Russell Lowell, and William Cullen Bryant. These poets preferred conventional styles and avoided experimentation. They addressed controversial issues of their time in their work in muted, romantic tones that appealed to reader's emotions rather than reason.

Longfellow was a literary giant in his time. In a time when it was extremely difficult to make any money from poetry, at one point the income Longfellow earned from his poetry rivaled what he earned at Harvard. But over the years, he fell out of favor, and his poetry was criticized for lacking emotional depth and failing to capture the vitality of the American spirit. It was as if Longfellow was too elegant, and his mastery of literary forms appeared too high-minded to embody the broadness of American cultural tastes. Longfellow's popularity and decline is a good lesson in how literature's appeal and values change over generations.

TRANSCENDENTALISM AND THE DARK ROMANTICS

Brooding Sisters

A very interesting thing began happening in the late eighteenth century in Europe, which, by the early nineteenth century, had made its way to America via a young Unitarian minister named Ralph Waldo Emerson. It was called romanticism, and it completely changed the face of the literary, political, and religious landscapes of the Western world.

"The charming landscape which I saw this morning, is indubitably made up of some twenty or thirty farms. Miller owns this field, Locke that, and Manning the woodland beyond. But none of them owns the landscape."

—Ralph Waldo Emerson, "Nature"

ROMANTICISM

Romanticism was a movement in ideas and literature that focused on nature, emotion, and the individual. It championed the goodness of humanity, people's direct connection with nature, and individual worth.

The English writers William Wordsworth (1770–1850) and Samuel Taylor Coleridge (1772–1834) opened the movement with their collection of poetry, *Lyrical Ballads*, published in 1798. The collection began with Coleridge's poem "The Rime of the Ancient Mariner" and ended with Wordsworth's poem "Tintern Abbey." This collection of poetry was lyrical and dramatic, used language "really used by men," and was highly emotional. Wordsworth and Coleridge declared in their preface that they wanted to trace the "primary laws of our nature" through the "incidents and situations from common life."

No longer satisfied with the strict rein the Enlightenment put on the mind to follow reason, structure, and order, and the heart to play second fiddle to the mind, the romanticists stressed the imaginative powers of the human mind and heart. In Europe and America, neoclassical poetry like Freneau's was washed aside, and writers like Longfellow infused the effusive drama and lyrical nature of the movement into their elegantly metered poetry.

TRANSCENDENTALISM

The movement took a unique shape in America in the form of transcendentalism, a small but long-lasting movement that changed the course of America's intellectual progress in the early nineteenth century. Ralph Waldo Emerson (1803–1882) took the ideas of the romantic era and blended them with his own new conception of the divinity in his short essay called "Nature" that ushered in the transcendental era and formed the basis for a new crop of writers and thinkers in the nineteenth century.

Transcendentalism held a core belief that the individual could "transcend" the physical world of the senses through intuition to reach an experience of God. Unlike Locke, who said the way to know God was through reason, or Jonathan Edwards, who endeavored to incite his parishioners to reach God through emotional experience, the transcendentalists believed that intuition alone was all one needed to achieve an experience of God.

Hawthorne and the Transcendentalists

The writer Nathaniel Hawthorne joined the ill-fated Brook Farm transcendental utopian commune begun in 1841 by the progressive Unitarian minister George Ripley (1802–1880). Hawthorne hoped to join the commune in order to save money to marry his wife, Sophia, but quickly became disillusioned with the project. He was assigned to shovel manure (affectionately referred to as the "Gold Mine"), and couldn't stand the job. He confided in Sophia that he didn't realize farming was so hard and that he desired to escape before his soul was "utterly buried in a dungheap." His distaste for transcendentalism lasted for the rest of his life.

Dark Romantics

A darker side of the romantic movement emerged in the nineteenth century as well: A core group of writers—Nathaniel Hawthorne, Herman Melville, and Edgar Allan Poe, among others—began writing about darker themes like sin, guilt, and evil. These writers were concerned with the darker aspects of the human heart, not content to accept the "sunnier" aspects of the romanticists and transcendentalists. They looked into the aspects of human nature that were difficult to face. They created new forms like the detective story and psychological novel to express their themes.

RALPH WALDO EMERSON

The Plato of America

Washington Irving and Henry Wadsworth Longfellow may have put America on the literary map, but it was Ralph Waldo Emerson who started filling in the details. With Emerson, America finally had its own literary father, its own "native" philosopher. Emerson turned Americans' heads toward their own literary future, establishing new ideals and shaping an entirely new American consciousness.

With the publication of his essay "Nature" in 1836, Emerson became the center of a literary and philosophical group now known as the American transcendentalists. These intellectuals, artists, and writers flocked to Emerson to hear what this "sage of Concord" had to say. They began meeting regularly in Boston to share ideas and parse out just what transcendentalism meant for the spirit and minds of American men and women. They collectively became known as the "Transcendental Club" (a derisive term at first). They used Emerson's essay "Nature" as their manifesto.

In this landmark essay Emerson lays out an entirely new intellectual and spiritual framework for the American. "Nature" is short, but it contains everything Emerson espoused throughout his life:

- The universe is composed of two things: nature and the soul.
- You are part of nature, and therefore a part of God.
- When you "commune" with nature you are communing with God. God does not exist separately from nature or from you.
- Nature can restore you to faith and reason.

Emerson composed the essay after a major breaking point in his young life. He had lost his first wife Ellen after only a few years of marriage. Emerson, who was a Unitarian minister, became disillusioned with the spiritual and intellectual traditions that were supposed to support him in this tender time of crisis. He referred to Boston's brand of Unitarianism as "corpse-cold" for its inability to address the spiritual and emotional needs of its parishioners. Grief-stricken and yearning for spiritual nourishment, he left for Europe.

Morbid Curiosity

Emerson was so unhinged by his wife's death that in a visit to her grave a year after she died, he opened her coffin to look inside.

Emerson came back refreshed and emboldened by his intellectual encounters abroad, which included introductions to Thomas Carlyle, and William Wordsworth and Samuel Taylor Coleridge, two of the major writers of the romantic period. These writers made a deep impact on him, as did new German philosophies that opened the Bible to literary interpretations rather than being simply holy scripture. Emerson wove all of these new ideas into a powerful new philosophical framework.

Emerson's "Nature" essay was important because it redefined spirituality for Americans and made the *individual* and personal *intuition* the center of spirituality, not reason or church doctrine. He writes that the way back to the root of our spirituality and creativity is through nature:

In the woods, we return to reason and faith. There I feel that nothing can befall me in life—no disgrace, no calamity, (leaving me my eyes), which nature cannot repair. Standing on the bare ground—my head bathed by the blithe air, and uplifted into infinite space—all mean egotism vanishes. I become a transparent eye-ball. I am nothing; I see all; the currents of the Universal Being circulate through me; I am part or particle of God.

This is a pretty heavy passage, and you could easily write volumes trying to unpack all of the meaning in it, but in essence, Emerson is saying one big thing: that in order to revitalize one's spirit, and truly understand the nature of God, one must retreat from society and all its trappings. Even religion, with all its formalities, can become a distraction, a barrier to understanding God. Where Jonathan Edwards before him tried to restore this type of ecstatic joy in the hearts of his parishioners by inciting their emotions with fear, Emerson does it by injecting a sense of joy and self-worth into the hearts of his readers.

Frogpondians

Not everyone was a fan of transcendentalism. Edgar Allan Poe gave followers of the movement the moniker "frogpondians" (after the Frog Pond on Boston Common) in his short story "Never Bet the Devil Your Head." Poe in particular didn't like the transcendentalist style of writing, which turned the so-called poetry of its ideas into the "flattest kind" of prose (he found it too highfalutin and wishy-washy).

Charged by Emerson's optimism, a new group of writers, intellectuals, and artists began creating works that prioritized the individual, creating a new American identity. Emerson continued to write over the next several years, expressing the practical aspects of transcendentalism in a series of lectures, speeches, and essays.

"THE AMERICAN SCHOLAR"

What would transcendentalism look like to the intellectual? Emerson gave his answer in an 1837 speech to the Phi Beta Kappa Society at Harvard titled "The American Scholar," a year after "Nature" was published. In his speech he urged the audience to trust their own intellect and the power of their own individuality, arguing, "We have listened too long to the courtly muses of Europe. . . . We will walk on our own feet; we will work with our own hands; we will speak our own minds." "Over-influence," he wrote "is the enemy of genius." He christened a new scholar, the "American Scholar," as one who would be brave enough to follow his or her intellect, and become a "Man thinking" not a "mere thinker," or "still worse, the parrot of other men's thinking." This exciting speech electrified minds, leading Oliver Wendell Holmes Sr., a prominent intellectual of the time, to call it America's "intellectual Declaration of Independence."

The Divinity School Address

What would transcendentalism look like when applied to the work of the clergyman? Emerson would give his answer to the graduating class of the Harvard Divinity School on July 15, 1838. In his address Emerson questioned the effect of religious doctrine, and argued that truth, and the beauty of God, are an institution unto themselves, outside of the walls of the church and the ministers that guard them. He wrote:

Before every man . . . the oracles of this truth cease never, it is guarded by one stern condition; this, namely; it is an institution. It cannot be received at second hand. Truly speaking, it is not instruction, but provocation, that I can receive from another soul.

To illustrate this point he tells an anecdote where he "once heard a preacher who sorely tempted me to say, I would go to church no more." He describes the scene inside the pews:

> A snow storm was falling around us. The snow storm was real; the preacher merely spectral; and the eye felt the sad contrast in looking at him, and then out of the window behind him, into the beautiful meteor of the snow.

To the Unitarians of Boston, Emerson's transcendental ideas sounded heretical—if an individual didn't need a minister to deliver and receive God, then church was unnecessary. Further, Emerson's ideas placed God outside in nature, not inside the protected walls of church. The speech enraged ministers, and Harvard banned Emerson from speaking at the school for thirty years.

"Self-Reliance"

Finally, what does transcendentalism look like to the average individual? From his essay "Self-Reliance," published in 1841, come some of Emerson's most well-known quotes, like: "Whoso would be a man must be a nonconformist," and "Nothing is at last sacred but the integrity of your own mind." The essay beams with Emerson's supreme confidence in the divinity of the individual. Emerson instructs the individual to "learn to detect and watch that gleam of light which flashes across his mind from within, more than the luster of the firmament of bards and sages." Emerson argues that for everyone, personal responsibility, nonconformity, and "self-reliance" are the way to lasting happiness and satisfaction.

While Emerson's reputation within the religious community fell sharply after the Divinity School Address, his reputation as a writer and thinker was just beginning. When he gave the Divinity School Address he was only thirty-five years old. For the remaining decades of his life, Emerson settled into a life as a prestigious essayist and lecturer, gaining legions of listeners and followers and establishing the basis of an American literature. With the publication of his two volumes of essays (*Essays: First Series* and *Essays: Second Series*), he had secured his enduring legacy as a prose stylist and thinker, and shaper of the American ideal.

HENRY DAVID THOREAU

Writer of Nature

Coming just behind Emerson as one of the most important writers and thinkers of the nineteenth century is Henry David Thoreau (1817–1862). He also lived in Concord and was a core member of Emerson's transcendentalists. He once said, "I have never got over my surprise that I should have been born into the most estimable place in all the world, and in the very nick of time, too." And it was true—he really was born at the right place, at the right time.

"Call Me Saunterer"

While twenty miles may seem like an awfully long distance to walk just to hear a lecture, for Thoreau it was all part of a day well spent. Thoreau had a lifelong habit of taking long walks, notoriously repelling offers to join him. He considered it a sacred art, capable of restoring a person to inner vitality.

No one knows for sure when Thoreau first met Emerson. One legend says it was when Thoreau walked to Boston from Concord (a distance of more than twenty miles!) to hear Emerson speak. When Emerson found out what he'd done, he invited the poor chap to his house to hear his lectures there. However it began, their friendship would go down as one of the most famous and enduring in literary history.

Thoreau was born in 1817 in Concord. Except for a brief stint in New York City and in Boston, he lived in Concord his entire life. He claimed he "traveled a good deal in Concord" and was indeed a keen observer of his beloved hometown. Thoreau attended Harvard from 1833 to 1837 and became a schoolteacher, but it didn't last long because he disagreed with the school's corporal punishment policies. For the rest of his life, he drifted career-wise, alternating between handyman, land surveyor, and working in his father's pencil business. His neighbors viewed him as an eccentric loafer, refusing to take a "real" job and settle down.

The Art of Living Well

Even Emerson wished Thoreau would apply his talents and take up a career, but in his eulogy, Emerson admits that Thoreau "declined to give up his large ambition of knowledge and action for any narrow craft or profession, aiming at a much more comprehensive calling, the art of living well."

At the age of twenty-eight, still grief-stricken by the death of his brother John, and desperately looking for purpose, Thoreau made a fateful decision to move to the shores of a pond in Concord called Walden.

Thoreau the Writer

Thoreau lived on the shores of Walden Pond from 1845 to 1847, on a parcel of land owned by Emerson. He built a small cabin (detailing the entire cost, down to the nails), furnished it with a desk, a bed, and a chair, and spent his days tending a small crop of beans, fishing in the pond, and writing—mostly a book memorializing a canoe trip he and his brother took down the Concord and Merrimack Rivers. Thoreau posed the experience as an experiment in simplicity, to "live deliberately, to front only the essential facts of life, and see if I could not learn what it had to teach, and not, when I came to die, discover that I had not lived a true account of it in my next excursion." He intended to show, by his experiment, how many things people considered necessary to their life were actually distractions and that one always has a choice to live a life of deliberate simplicity.

Thoreau gives a full account of his experience in his book *Walden*, his masterpiece. The book is a fine example of transcendentalist writing with its characteristic use of aphorisms, paradox, poetic prose, and mix of philosophy, social criticism, and literary allusion. Essentially, *Walden* is a massive handbook on how to live—and wisely. Thoreau's *Walden* became a manifesto on materialism in American culture, still used as an antidote to the ills of consumerism and spiritual decay today.

Master of Paradox

Like Emerson, Thoreau is one of the most quotable American writers. Thoreau was a master of the tightly crafted aphoristic and paradoxical line. Lines such as, "We do not ride on the railroad; it rides upon us," and "Heaven is under our feet as well as over our heads" capture the essence of transcendentalist thought.

Thoreau, the Political Critic

After Thoreau came back from his "retreat," he found himself looking at a world on fire over war and slavery. When the Mexican-American War broke out, Thoreau was outraged. The war aimed to tip the scale toward slave-owning states in the Union. Thoreau refused to pay a poll tax that year on the principle that he could not support a government that supported slavery. Because of his refusal, he was put in jail.

A Night in Jail

Reflecting on the incident, Thoreau penned one of his most famous political essays, "Resistance to Civil Government." He argued that individuals should never let government actions override their consciences, and that "under a government which imprisons unjustly, the true place for a just man is also a prison." He declared, "If a thousand men were not to pay their tax bills this year, that would not be a violent and bloody measure, as it would be to pay them, and enable the State to commit violence and shed innocent blood. This is, in fact, the definition of a peaceable revolution, if any such is possible."

Civil Disobedience

Gandhi and Martin Luther King Jr. later used Thoreau's powerful essay as a cornerstone document for their nonviolent resistance movements. King writes in his *The Autobiography of Martin Luther King Jr.*, "I became convinced that noncooperation with evil is as much a moral obligation as is cooperation with good. No other person has been more eloquent and passionate in getting this idea across than Henry David Thoreau. As a result of his writings and personal witness, we are the heirs of a legacy of creative protest."

"A Plea for Captain John Brown"

Thoreau once again put pen to paper to express his rage over political events in 1859, after John Brown committed his infamous raid on Harpers Ferry. Disgusted by the press's characterization of Brown as insane, Thoreau compared Brown to Christ, and Brown's execution to the execution of Christ by Pontius Pilate. Thoreau boldly declared Brown a "hero" saying, "I think that for once the

Sharp's rifles and the revolvers were employed in a righteous cause. The tools were in the hands of one who could use them." In this fiery, finger-pointing lecture, Thoreau censured the public for not recognizing the divinity in Brown's last speech before he was hanged: "You don't know your testament when you see it."

John Brown's Raid on Harpers Ferry

On October 16, 1859, John Brown and twenty-one of his followers attempted to raid a federal arsenal in Harpers Ferry, Virginia, to arm a slave rebellion. His plan failed, and ten of his men were killed while he was captured. Brown was found guilty of treason and hanged on December 2, 1859. The events of Harpers Ferry inflamed both sides of the slavery issue and contributed to the outbreak of the Civil War.

A True Transcendentalist

In "A Plea for Captain John Brown" we get a glimpse of Thoreau's definition of a transcendentalist: "A man of rare common sense and directness of speech, as of action: a transcendentalist above all, a man of ideas and principles—that was what distinguished him. Not yielding to a whim or transient impulse, but carrying out the purpose of a life."

THOREAU THE SCIENTIST

Throughout his life, Thoreau was an acute observer of the natural world, sometimes spending an entire day watching just one spot in a river. At one point, Louis Agassiz, a leading biologist and geologist at Harvard at the time, enlisted Thoreau to help collect specimens for him. Thoreau's keen observations of nature led him to develop his own scientific theories later in his life, including his theory of the dispersal of seeds documented in his essay "The Succession of Forest Trees." He was also one of the first readers of Charles Darwin's *The Voyage of the Beagle*.

Using Thoreau's Journals

Scientists are now using Thoreau's journals to study climate change. His careful chronicles of when flowers bloomed, leaves turned colors, and other signs of seasonal change help scientists understand how the climate has changed since his time.

When Thoreau died, he was viewed as a minor disciple of Emerson. He is now seen as a literary and philosophical giant in his own right. He is recognized as a brilliant prose stylist, a radical political philosopher, a sharp social critic, and the father of the environmental conservation movement. History is full of people who mark as a turning point in their lives when they first read Thoreau and who make pilgrimages to Walden Pond hoping to catch a spark of the divinity of nature Thoreau spoke so well of.

NATHANIEL HAWTHORNE

Exposing the Dark Side of America

Imagine, if you will, an enormous, dark manse in nineteenth-century New England. Inside, brooding in one of the back corners of a dimly lit room, is a pondering writer who will become one of the most famous chroniclers of guilt, sin, and the deeper recesses of the soul in American literary history. There you have Nathaniel Hawthorne (1804–1864), the man who put a big scarlet "A" over our literary hearts, and created an unlikely American heroine, Hester Prynne.

In the introduction to his famous work, *The Scarlet Letter*, Nathaniel Hawthorne writes:

Moonlight, in a familiar room, falling so white upon the carpet, and showing all its figures so distinctly—making every object so minutely visible, yet so unlike a morning or noontide visibility—is a medium the most suitable for a romance-writer to get acquainted with his illusive guests. There is the little domestic scenery of the well-known apartment; the chairs, with each its separate individuality; the centre-table, sustaining a work-basket, a volume or two, and an extinguished lamp; the sofa; the book-case; the picture on the wall;—all these details, so completely seen, are so spiritualized by the unusual light, that they seem to lose their actual substance, and become things of intellect. . . . Thus, therefore the floor of our familiar room has become a neutral territory, somewhere between the real world and fairy-land, where the Actual and the Imaginary may meet, and each imbue itself with the nature of the other.

This is Hawthorne's signal to his readers that they are *not* about to read just any garden-variety novel. They are going to read a *romance*, a genre of writing where the "Actual and the Imaginary" (may) meet to create something otherworldly, something richly imaginative, but still very much real.

It's not surprising that Hawthorne chose moonlight falling across a domestic scene to describe his brand of romance: Hawthorne was a hermit and spent many hours holed up in his rooms. Until age thirty-three, he lived in a sort of self-imposed exile in his mother's house, intent on becoming the nation's next great writer. Once he actually did become a famous writer, he shrewdly capitalized on his quirky personality, cultivating a persona of the shy literary recluse. The truth was he *was* a painfully shy person all of his life and hell-bent on making it in the literary world.

Not Quite

In those dozen years Hawthorne spent at home after college he produced a novel called *Fanshawe*, which he self-published in 1828. Embarrassed, he quickly retracted it, recognizing it as a mawkish effort of an inexperienced writer.

A Winning Combination

Hawthorne found his winning combination when he set his romance of sin and guilt, *The Scarlet Letter*, in colonial Salem. At the time critics had been encouraging fiction writers to use colonial history to create "native" novels that were truly American. Lydia Maria Child had set her romance, *Hobomok*, published in 1824, in colonial Salem, and Hawthorne followed suit. Unlike Child, however, Hawthorne had a personal connection to colonial Salem—his ancestor

John Hathorne was a judge who participated in the infamous Salem witch trials and was notably the only judge who never repented. The Hathorne family was so ashamed of this fact that they added a *w* to the family name to distance themselves from their family's involvement.

The Scarlet *A* of Shame

The Scarlet Letter follows the story of Hester Prynne, a Puritan woman who becomes pregnant and gives birth to a baby named Pearl while her husband is away in England. The Puritan community forces her to the scaffold to confess her sin, making her wear a scarlet letter "A" (for adulterer) as a symbol of her sin.

When Hester's husband, Roger Chillingworth, returns to the community, he launches an obsessive search for Pearl's father, learning that it is—ironically—the Reverend Arthur Dimmesdale. Chillingworth's maniacal hunt for Dimmesdale wears on Dimmesdale's soul, and his guilt manifests physically, eventually killing him. Chillingworth becomes wrecked from the debacle. Hester is the only one who comes out clean, growing from the ordeal and reconciling herself with God.

The romance is America's first psychological novel, masterfully blending allegory with the universal themes of guilt and sin. The novel addressed some of the spiritual and moral issues of the time, the ones that stemmed from Americans' Puritan heritage. Hawthorne approached the themes from what he considered a standpoint of "truth," unafraid to face the darker aspects of the faith.

TWISTED HOUSE

Shortly after *The Scarlet Letter* was published, Hawthorne published another novel, *The House of the Seven Gables*, in 1851. The work was also set in Salem and also inspired by his family history. The novel took place in a gabled home, which was based on one in Salem that was owned by relatives of Hawthorne's. Hawthorne once again explored themes of guilt and sin, this time mixed with supernatural elements like witchcraft and curses.

In the novel, Colonel Pyncheon fraudulently seizes property from Matthew Maule, a man accused of witchcraft and sentenced to death. Maule places a curse on the Pyncheon family before he dies, and at the colonel's housewarming party, guests find Pyncheon dead in his armchair. Like Dimmesdale's body in *The Scarlet Letter*, the house erodes over time, weighed by the wrongful doings of its owners.

I'M A HAPPY PERSON, REALLY!

Despite his penchant for dark, psychological themes, Hawthorne led a happy life with his wife Sophia. During their marriage, Hawthorne settled into a long period of relative stability during which he created his best works. They exchanged some beautiful love letters and had a big family. His wife was devastated when she learned he died of a heart attack in 1864 while on a walking tour in New Hampshire with his friend, the former president, Franklin Pierce.

Hawthorne's Legacy

Hawthorne exposed the darker sides of America's past in richly complex, psychological dramas. Where others were trying to wrest a sense of the optimism and innate goodness of human nature from the prison of America's Puritan past, Hawthorne faced the realities of human failings with a piercing investigative eye. He laid out the devastating effects of guilt on the psyche with his characters, but also the redemptive power of sympathy for the natural human passions.

Hawthorne won a friend in another writer, Herman Melville, for his efforts, and they both shared a reputation as America's "dark" writers of the romantic period. After the romantic era expanded who could be considered an "author," much less what could be considered a "novel," both writers claimed their space in the *romance* genre, where they could bring more fantastical elements to their writing while still maintaining that their works were realistic narratives.

HERMAN MELVILLE

America's Dark Romantic

Any struggling author today might find consolation in knowing that Herman Melville (1819–1891) didn't have it so easy, either. Melville's story of literary success and failure is as common now as it was in his time: An author makes a splash on the literary scene, the public demands more of the same, but the author has moved on. His growth as an artist no longer lets him produce the same type of work, the public rejects him, and his star fades. This is how we understand Melville today—as a misunderstood genius whose star extended far wider than the circumference of his public's taste.

Travel Narratives in the Nineteenth Century

Travel narratives were one of the most popular genres in the nineteenth century. Both educational and entertaining, "adventure" narratives provided a glimpse into the behaviors, customs, and beliefs of the outside world. Americans were fascinated learning about foreign cultures, especially as a way to understand their own place in the world.

A WHALE OF A TIME

We know Melville now for his whale of a masterpiece, *Moby-Dick*, but in his time, it was his two first works, *Typee* and *Omoo*, for which he was most famous. Melville wrote *Typee*, an autobiographical travel narrative based on his experience being held captive by cannibals after he deserted the whaling ship *Acushnet* in 1841. The cannibals on the Marquesas Islands were fortunately friendly, fun-loving cannibals, and Melville was able to leave and find his way back home months later. People were captivated by the exotic story, and the book made Melville an immediate success. He followed up with *Omoo*, a book of more of his tales from the Polynesian islands. It appeared Melville had a long road of literary fame ahead of him.

I Want Romance

Buoyed by new fame, a new wife, and a blossoming friendship with the writer Nathaniel Hawthorne, Melville began writing another work, *Mardi*, which was published in 1849. Like Hawthorne, Melville was now interested in writing *romance*, in which he could be free to write a work based on symbolic representations of ideas rather than the facts of his real life.

Mardi was a precursor to *Moby-Dick* in that it was an allegory centered on a philosophical quest. The book was panned by critics and rejected by the public, who just wanted to hear more exciting sea adventures. Dejected, Melville wrote to his friend Hawthorne, "What I feel most moved to write, that is banned. It will not pay. Yet altogether, write the *other* way I cannot. So the product is a final hash, and all my books are botches."

The Tale of the Whale

Melville's masterpiece, *Moby-Dick*, in many ways is a hash—it is a mix of styles, narrative points of view, and literary forms. It contains dictionary entries; word etymologies; whaling manual entries; elaborate, contorted sentence structures; and biblical allusions. It is part comedy, part tragedy, and part epic (and very long!). For all its complexity, the book is a masterful mix of all of these features.

Moby-Dick opens with one of the most famous lines in literature: "Call me Ishmael." Ishmael, the narrator of the book, decides he has had enough of land for the time and joins the crew of a whaling ship, the *Pequod*. As he waits to set sail, he finds himself sharing a room at an inn with another crewmember, Queequeg, a cannibal and harpooneer from the South Seas. They don't meet their mysterious captain, Ahab, until after the ship sets sail. Ahab announces to the crew that this will not be a run-of-the-mill whaling trip—they are on a mission to find a formidable white whale named Moby Dick, which once claimed Ahab's leg in a violent attack. The crew is now part of Ahab's monomaniacal quest to avenge his attack. They encounter Moby Dick three times, until the great White Whale finally crushes the ship, taking Ahab down with it into the vortex of the sea after the rope of Ahab's harpoon catches his own neck. Ishmael is the only crewmember who survives to tell the tale, floating atop Queequeg's coffin.

In His Own Words

In his own words, Captain Ahab reveals the reasons behind his mad quest:

> "All visible objects, man, are but as pasteboard masks. . . . If man will strike, strike through the mask! How can the prisoner reach outside except by thrusting through the wall? To me, the white whale is that wall, shoved near to me. . . . He tasks me; he heaps me; I see in him outrageous strength, with an inscrutable malice sinewing in it. That inscrutable thing is chiefly what I hate; and be the white whale agent, or be the white whale principal, I will wreak that hate upon him."

At its base *Moby-Dick* is an allegorical quest narrative, but the complexity of the book lends itself to many interpretations: Some read it as a cautionary tale of the hubris of man to try to control nature, some see Ahab's mission to kill Moby Dick as a fight against evil (Moby Dick = evil), some see it as both Ahab's and Ishmael's search for the meaning of life (Moby Dick = God or God's indifference). For both Ahab and Ishmael, the whale is the center of the book, a mysterious gigantic creature that symbolizes the ineffableness of nature. Both try to come to terms with the whale—Ahab with his harpoon and Ishmael with his exhaustive lists of whale anatomies, dictionary of whaling terms, and passages clipped from whaling manuals.

The Outcast

Ishmael is the name of the outcast son of Abraham in the book of Genesis. By using the name *Ishmael*, Melville casts his narrator as a kind of outcast of society.

Down the Whirlpool

Moby-Dick made barely a ripple when it was published—it took more than seventy years for it to come into its own, finally recognized as the literary masterpiece it is. Hawthorne, to whom the book was dedicated, was one of the few people who praised the book.

Melville never recaptured his fame after *Typee* and *Omoo*, and for the rest of his life he worked largely unnoticed, bitter that the only way for him to sustain himself through his writing would be to pander to the public's taste. Many of his works after *Moby-Dick*, such as the short story "Bartleby, the Scrivener," a parable about how commerce and the human spirit are incompatible, and *The Confidence-Man*, a book satirizing the level of faith people like Emerson put in the goodness of human nature, are testaments to his bitterness. Melville died relatively unknown but has now become recognized as the author of (in some minds) "the great American novel."

Literature with Coffee

The next time you go to pick up that cup of Starbucks, think of this fun fact: Starbucks coffee is named after Starbuck, the first mate of the illustrious *Pequod*.

EDGAR ALLAN POE

His Tell-Tale Heart

He created the modern detective story and the modern short story, inspired a league of pop-culture psychological thrillers, and wrote one of the most famous poems in American literature. His name is synonymous with the macabre, and the raven. He is Edgar Allan Poe (1809–1849).

POE'S EARLY LIFE

Poe's life was almost as dramatic as his writing. He was born to two actors, but his father abandoned the family when Poe was two years old, and his mother died shortly after. Poe was thus orphaned as a small boy. Luckily, a wealthy merchant from Virginia named John Allan took the boy in and formally named him "Edgar Allan Poe."

Allan sent Poe to the University of Virginia, but Poe got into trouble almost as soon as his father dropped him off at the college gates. Poe was forced to leave college after accumulating a giant pile of gambling debts by the end of his first year. He split and left for Boston, determined to make a career as a writer.

CLIMBING THE LADDER OF SUCCESS . . . SORT OF

Poe self-published a collection called *Tamerlane and Other Poems*, but it was not a commercial success. He eventually left Boston for

Baltimore to connect with relatives, and ended up living with his aunt and her daughter, Virginia. He secretly married his cousin in 1835 when Virginia was only thirteen years old and Poe was twenty-six.

Poe didn't abandon his dream of making a career as a writer and spent the next decade moving between major literary centers of the Eastern Seaboard, New York, Philadelphia, Baltimore, and Richmond, with varied success. He never made a comfortable living with his writing and notoriously died in an alleyway in mysterious circumstances. Against a backdrop of drama and poverty, he managed to create his legacy.

Poe's major works fall into three main categories—literary criticism, poetry, and fiction. Here's how each breaks down:

Literary Criticism
Signature work: "The Philosophy of Composition"
We now most associate Poe with the gothic short story, but during his time he was also known for his literary criticism. He was one of the few writers of his time to predict Longfellow's decline, which gained him the respect of some critics. He used his own work as the subject of his essay "The Philosophy of Composition," where he established rules for poetry. He argued a poem should:

- Be able to be read in one sitting ("if two sittings be required, the affairs of the world interfere, and every thing like totality is at once destroyed.")
- Be concerned with beauty over truth ("pleasure . . . most pure, is, . . . found in the contemplation of the beautiful.")
- Not be concerned with teaching a lesson
- Be concerned with effect over realistic details ("Beauty is the sole legitimate province of the poem.")

In setting down these rules, Poe essentially created the argument for the short story as well.

Poetry
Signature work: "The Raven"

Here is the first stanza of Poe's famous poem "The Raven" (try reading it aloud!):

Once upon a midnight dreary, while I pondered, weak and weary,
Over many a quaint and curious volume of forgotten lore—
While I nodded, nearly napping, suddenly there came a tapping,
As of someone gently rapping, rapping at my chamber door.
"'Tis some visitor," I muttered, "tapping at my chamber door—
Only this and nothing more."

The Jingle Man

Not everyone was a fan of "The Raven." Ralph Waldo Emerson's reaction to it? "I see nothing in it." He gave Poe the moniker "the jingle man," finding the emphasis on sound and rhythm in the poem excessive.

"The Raven" is an eighteen-stanza ballad in which the poet falls into madness mourning the death of his love, Lenore. A raven (real or imagined) taunts the poet by repeatedly uttering one word: "Nevermore." The strong rhythm of the poem echoes Poe's belief that poetry should be pleasurable and create an effect in the reader.

A ballad is a form of lyric poetry that usually tells a story and was often set to music. Ballads have a characteristically musical quality to them. Many pop songs (especially love songs) are ballads.

Other notable poems by Poe include "Annabel Lee," "The City in the Sea," and "To Helen."

Fiction
Signature works: "The Tell-Tale Heart" and "The Gold-Bug"

"True!" begins "The Tell-Tale Heart," Poe's most famous short story. The story is one of the finest examples of gothic fiction.

This very short story is told by a murderer trying to convince the reader that he is not insane. The murderer recounts how he dismembered his victim's body (his landlord's, whom he was convinced had an "evil eye"), and hid it under the floorboards of his room. When the police come to investigate, everything goes well until the narrator hears what he thinks is the beating heart of his victim:

> It grew louder—louder—louder! And still the men chatted pleasantly, and smiled. Was it possible they heard not? Almighty God!—no, no! They heard—they suspected!—they knew—they were making a mockery of my horror!

The murderer, agonized, tears up the floorboards and confesses to the crime. The man's guilt has manifested as the sound of his victim's beating heart. This psychological component became a signature element in Poe's work.

The First Detective Story

Poe's short story "The Gold-Bug" was markedly different from his horror tales such as "The Tell-Tale Heart." With the "The Gold-Bug," Poe established the detective story, a genre in which a mystery is solved. Poe's characters are rational, and the story contains much less emphasis on psychological drama than on the process by which the mystery (the discovery of a vast buried treasure) is resolved.

Other notable short stories by Poe include "The Masque of the Red Death," "The Cask of Amontillado," and "The Purloined Letter."

Poe's aesthetic philosophies, which emphasize effect over reason and prioritize emotion and psychological themes, place him within the romantic tradition of his era, but like Nathaniel Hawthorne and Herman Melville, he is classed as a "dark romantic" for his fascination with melancholy and the darker sides of the human heart. While Poe enjoyed a fair amount of attention during his time, his reputation wasn't firmly established until after he died and his contributions to literature were more obvious.

Chapter 4

Literature of the Civil War

By 1855, it was becoming clear that America was heading toward its next crisis. The explosion of new technologies that had emerged during the Industrial Revolution that were beginning to take shape in America now threatened to divide it. The North was quickly becoming the industrial hub of the nation as it embraced inventions such as the steam engine, railroad, and steam printing press. The South, in contrast, was slower to embrace these new inventions. As wonderful as the new technologies were, their economic benefits, in the eyes of Southerners, still did not outweigh those of the slave system. As a result, the South remained largely agricultural as the North moved forward toward manufacturing.

As the North became more industrialized, it became more attuned to human rights issues and grew increasingly intolerant of slavery. Abolitionists in the North decried the abuses of slavery and called for an end to the slave system. The indictment of slavery that had been stricken from Thomas Jefferson's first draft of the Declaration of Independence had now exploded into a full-on social reform movement. This enraged the South, which viewed these calls as a direct threat to its economy.

These arguments had an enormous effect on literature. Writers galvanized by the issue of slavery produced a fiery new crop of speeches, narratives, political tracts, and novels that explored slavery's emotional, spiritual, political, and economic costs to the nation. Writers such as Harriet Beecher Stowe, Frederick Douglass, and Lydia Maria Child wrote works that both helped shape the country's thought and drive it apart. All the while two writers, Walt Whitman and Emily Dickinson, were quietly at work on a poetry that would revolutionize American literature in the decades to come.

HARRIET BEECHER STOWE

The Lady Who Started a Great Big War

By the end of its first year of publication, *Uncle Tom's Cabin* by Harriet Beecher Stowe (1811–1896) was a bona fide bestseller. On its first day alone it sold 3,000 copies, and by the end of its first year in publication it had sold 350,000 copies, making it the bestselling book in American history. By 1860, eight years after its publication as a book, it had been translated into twenty-three languages and had gone through several editions in Europe. At one point, the Bible was the only book that was selling more copies! This lone book from the pen of an obscure woman in Maine had managed to incite extreme outrage and praise, and plunged the fragile Union into an all-out war of words over slavery.

STOWE MEETS LINCOLN

People often say *Uncle Tom's Cabin* helped ignite the Civil War. One legend has it that Abraham Lincoln, upon meeting Stowe at the beginning of the Civil War, said to her, "So this is the little lady who started this great war." (It's probably not true.)

Uncle Tom and His Cabin

So what is *Uncle Tom's Cabin* about and how did it start a war? The book tells the stories of two slaves—one affectionately called Uncle Tom and another named Eliza. Because of debts incurred by the plantation owner, Mr. Shelby, Tom and Harry (Eliza's son) are to be sold from the Kentucky plantation where they have worked most of their lives. Their lives take different turns; Uncle Tom accepts his fate and is sent to his new owner. Eliza, however, frenzied by the knowledge that her son will be separated from her, decides to escape. Tom, after the death of his new master, ends up in the hands of Simon Legree, a brutal slave owner (and one of the most cruel characters in American literature) who eventually beats him to death. Eliza meets up with her husband and safely escapes to Canada with their son.

Stop: You're Being Pulled Over for a Literary Offense

It hasn't been all smooth sailing for Stowe's reputation: Critics of the book have criticized Stowe for propagating stereotypes about black people and for casting Tom as a Christ-like dutiful Christian, passively loyal to his masters even in the face of their brutality. The critics don't like passages like this:

"I've lost everything,—wife, and children, and home, and a kind Mas'r,—and he would have set me free, if he'd only lived a week longer; I've lost everything in *this* world, and it's clean gone, forever,—and now I *can't* lose Heaven, too; no, I can't get to be wicked, besides all!"

In the passage, Tom is tempted to turn on his masters but replies that despite all of his suffering he cannot lose his Christian nature. Another literary offense, detractors point out, is the book's overly complicated plot. People have seen it as simply a vehicle to drive the political messages of the book.

Uncle Tom's Cabin: The Political Background

Stowe wrote the book after becoming enraged about the passage of the Fugitive Slave Act in 1850. Many Northerners shared Stowe's outrage at the passage of the act, which criminalized anyone who helped an escaped slave. The act was a political compromise meant to ease the growing tensions between the North and South; however, it tore them apart.

Southern states, in contrast, were slower to admit that slavery was immoral, claiming it was a "right" to own slaves. Anti-slavery sentiments steadily grew in the 1800s, and pressure built to find a resolution between the North and South over the issue. Northerners had a long history of helping escaped slaves from Southern states. Once the Fugitive Slave Act was passed, Northerners were now forced to be complicit in the institution of slavery.

Moving Away from Slavery

As early as 1787, several Northern states including Pennsylvania, New Hampshire, Massachusetts, Rhode Island, and Connecticut were already moving to abolish slavery in their states, acknowledging the moral issues slavery posed.

Stowe Connects Over Suffering

The issue of slavery had bothered Harriet Beecher Stowe for many years. She grew up in Cincinnati and had come in contact with many fugitive slaves as they crossed into Ohio from the neighboring slave state of Kentucky. Tales from Stowe's aunt, Mary Hubbard, whose husband owned a plantation in Jamaica and treated his slaves brutally, affected Stowe deeply. When Stowe lost her baby, Samuel, to cholera before he was a year old, her child's death connected her with the cause of slavery on an even more personal level; now she had even greater knowledge of the suffering slaves endured.

Stowe's father, Lyman Beecher, was an Evangelical Calvinist minister who encouraged his children (daughters included) to become evangelical workers. Encouraged by her aunt, Stowe decided to finally make her mark on the world—in the form of a book on the institution of slavery. Her intention was to write a book that would "awaken sympathy and feeling for the African race," and help people "feel right" about the issue of slavery. She appealed to readers' emotions, and used a heavily sentimental and realistic style of writing.

It's the System, Not the People

The book wasn't necessarily intended as a political piece of anti-slavery writing, or much less a carefully reasoned piece of abolitionist writing. In fact, much to the Northern abolitionists' chagrin, Stowe felt that it was the *system* of slavery, and not the slave owners themselves, that was the problem. Stowe's intentions were more religious and emotional than political in nature. Whatever Stowe's thoughts, the book exacerbated the tensions between the North and the South and blew open the issue of slavery. Now everyone's lips were on fire with the polemic of pro- and anti-slavery statements. In the South, people read the book as incendiary propaganda, and in the North, people read it as moral romance.

Our "Peculiar Institution"

Politicians, especially those in the South, used the euphemism "peculiar institution" to refer to the institution of slavery, preferring it to the term *slavery*, which was considered distasteful.

A Woman Abolitionist

With the success of the book, Stowe became an instant celebrity and the most famous woman in her day. She was invited to speak in America and in Europe and used her podium to speak against slavery.

At the time, it was shocking for women to speak publicly on divisive political issues like slavery. Angry Southerners called her intentions into question and accused her of fabricating stories of slave brutality. To silence her critics she wrote *A Key to Uncle Tom's Cabin*, which documented real cases of slave abuse. Through the strength of her intellect, she created a public space for women to speak on political affairs.

For all its failings as a sturdy piece of literature, *Uncle Tom's Cabin*'s overwhelming success at driving the public conversation on slavery and raising it to a fevered pitch has secured its reputation as an important book in American literature.

FREDERICK DOUGLASS

The Reality of Slavery

The same year Harriet Beecher Stowe's *Uncle Tom's Cabin* whipped up a frenzy over slavery, an ex-slave named Frederick Douglass (1818–1895) gave one of the most powerful orations on slavery in American history. It was called "What to a Slave Is the Fourth of July?" and it was delivered to a group of women at the Ladies' Anti-Slavery Society in Rochester, New York, on July 5, 1852.

A PAINFUL IRONY

In Douglass's carefully drafted speech, he poses a difficult question to his audience: "Do you mean, citizens, to mock me, by asking me to speak to-day?" Douglass explains, "The Fourth of July is yours, not mine. You may rejoice, I must mourn. To drag a man in fetters into the grand illuminated temple of liberty, and to call upon him to join you in joyous anthems, were inhuman mockery and sacrilegious irony." That likely left a few of those women squirming in their seats a bit.

Douglass's Early Life

Frederick Augustus Washington Bailey was born in Tuckahoe, Maryland, around 1817. His mother, Harriet Bailey, was a black slave. It was never publicly declared who Douglass's father was, but it was presumed he was his mother's white master, Aaron Anthony.

After his master's death in 1826, Douglass was sent to Baltimore, Maryland, to live with Hugh and Sophia Auld as a family servant. Sophia began giving Douglass reading lessons but was forced to stop after her husband found out. Her husband felt, as many people did at the time, that teaching slaves to read would make them unfit to be slaves. In fact, in many places in the South it was considered an offense to teach slaves to read.

A Soulless Practice

During slavery, it was common practice to separate slave babies from their parents to prevent any bonding between them that might interfere with their "management." Douglass was denied a relationship with his mother—most of his memories of her were from when she would come to sleep by his side every night and disappear in the morning.

Desperate to Learn

Douglass found ways to continue his studies by secretly enlisting the help of the white boys in the neighborhood to give him lessons. Douglass later reflected on the boys' help, saying, "I am strongly tempted to give the names of two or three of those little boys, as a testimonial of the gratitude and affection I bear them; but prudence forbids—not that it would injure me, but it might embarrass them; for it is almost an unpardonable offense to teach slaves to read in this Christian country."

A Slave Rises Up

At fifteen, for not working fast enough, Douglass was sent to work with a "slave breaker" named Edward Covey. Douglass described Covey as a "cruel man, hardened by a long life of slave-holding. He would at times seem to take great pleasure in whipping a slave." Covey whipped Douglass for months until Douglass fought back one day, overcoming Covey in a fight that lasted over two hours. He later recounted that he "resolved to fight . . . and as I did so, I rose." Shortly after the event, Douglass escaped to the North.

A New Life

Douglass had a difficult time when he first arrived in the North—single, alone, and without a place to stay. He met another woman slave with whom he had kept a correspondence for years, Anna Murray. They eventually married and settled in New Bedford, where Frederick changed his last name to "Douglass" to hide his identity.

Douglass Meets His Mentor

While in New England, Douglass met William Lloyd Garrison, the fiery center of the anti-slavery and abolitionist movement in the nineteenth century. Douglass began reading Garrison's abolitionist newspaper the *Liberator*, finding it so nourishing to his soul he called it his "food."

Not to Be Messed With

Garrison was extremely outspoken: In the first issue of the *Liberator* he wrote, "I do not wish to think, or speak, or write, with moderation . . . I WILL BE HEARD."

Garrison instantly recognized Douglass's potential as a speaker and invited him to represent the American Anti-Slavery Society. Douglass became a celebrity lecturer, captivating audiences with his eloquent and powerful delivery. He even went to lecture in Europe for two years (partly to protect himself—he was still legally a fugitive slave), recounting his stories of the brutality of slavery. The abolition movement now had a formidable spokesperson for the cause.

A Masterful Speaker Is Born

What did all that *look*, *sound*, and *feel* like? Here are a few memorable firsthand accounts:

"I shall never forget his first speech at the convention—the extraordinary emotion it excited in my own mind—the powerful impression it created upon a crowded auditory, completely taken by surprise—the applause which followed from the beginning to the end of his felicitous remarks. I think I never hated slavery so intensely as at that moment..."

—William Lloyd Garrison, from the preface to *Narrative of the Life of Fredrick Douglass*

"He was more than six feet in height, and his majestic form, as he rose to speak, straight as an arrow, muscular, yet lithe and graceful, his flashing eye, and more than all, his voice, that rivaled [Daniel] Webster's in its richness, and in the depth and sonorousness of its cadences, made up such an ideal of an orator as the listeners never forgot."

—Anonymous observer

Douglass was a master at conveying pathos to his listeners. At an anti-slavery meeting in 1842, he presented himself to the audience as a "thief and a robber," claiming he "stole this head, these limbs, this body from my master and ran off with them" to be with them to speak. His vivid, emotional descriptions of slavery arrested listeners' attentions.

A Masterful Writer Is Born

Douglass began to collect his stories into a book called the *Narrative of the Life of Frederick Douglass, an American Slave, Written by Himself*, which was published in 1845 by the American Anti-Slavery Society (with a preface by Garrison). The book electrified the abolitionist movement with its vivid detail and eloquent, highly developed style. His *Narrative* not only became one of the most famous slave narratives in American history but also one of the most famous autobiographies in American history.

Rhetorical Writing

In rhetorical writing, writers have many techniques to choose from to build and support their case. Douglass's speech follows a classic argumentative style in which a writer introduces a topic, states facts, offers arguments and counterarguments, and then reaches a conclusion. Douglass relies on irony to support the themes in his speech. His command of rhetoric further supports his case that African Americans were as intelligent as whites and deserved to be treated as equals.

DOUGLASS FINDS TRUE INDEPENDENCE

Ultimately Garrison's radicalism caused a rift between Douglass and Garrison. Garrison felt that virtually all institutions were corrupt—including churches and political parties—and felt the anti-slavery movement should not align itself with any institution. Even more, Garrison felt the Constitution was a pro-slavery document and that the Union should be dissolved.

Douglass's experiences abroad allowed him space to breathe and develop his own views, and his thinking became more pragmatic.

Douglass began thinking that the Constitution was *not* pro-slavery and could be "wielded" in the service of emancipation. He did not want the Union to dissolve since it would isolate the Southern slaves. Garrison felt betrayed and attacked Douglass bitterly in the *Liberator*. Their rift lasted beyond the Civil War and marked a key divide in anti-slavery thinking.

Douglass: Freedom Fighter for *All* People

Douglass continued his work on behalf of African Americans, but also worked on behalf of women as well: He attended the first women's rights convention in 1848 and supported the women's movement throughout his life. He also fought for the rights of Native Americans. He has gone down in history as one of the most powerful spokespersons of freedom.

LYDIA MARIA CHILD

Educating the Public Mind

Lydia Maria Child (1802–1880) may have begun her career as a fiction writer, but she ended it as one of the most powerful writers and educators of the abolitionist cause in the nineteenth century. Child became a formidable social critic whose writings spanned the gamut of human rights issues. No matter the topic, Child's primary role was as an "educator of public opinion": She aimed to educate, neutralize, and direct public opinion on the rights issues that blazed through America in the nineteenth century.

ABOLITIONIST BEGINNINGS

Born into an abolitionist family in Medford, Massachusetts, in 1802, Child was the youngest of six children. Her older brother Convers, who later became a clergyman and professor at Harvard Divinity School, was a major influence on Child's life. Convers exposed Child to major English writers such as Milton, Scott, Gibbon, and Shakespeare, and encouraged his younger sister to become a writer.

In 1821, Child read a review in the respected literary magazine *North American Review* in which a critic suggested fiction writers use New England colonial history as their subject matter. Inspired by the critic's suggestion, Child began writing her first book, *Hobomok*, a novel set in colonial Salem, which followed the story of a Native American who nobly and painfully walks away from his white wife Mary once they discover that her husband is not dead as they believed.

A Fearless Pen

The romance, published in 1825, became one of the first novels to "Americanize" the historical fiction genre invented by the English literary giant Sir Walter Scott in the nineteenth century. The book did more than spearhead a new genre and showcase Child's talents as a literary writer, however; it revealed glimmerings of her fearless pen. The subject of mixed-race marriage between the characters in *Hobomok* marked the start of Child's career as an outspoken writer of controversial topics and social reform.

Child, the "Every-Mom"

In her twenties, Child's writings mostly focused on children, women, and education. She began editing a monthly children's magazine called *The Juvenile Miscellany* that featured stories, poems, history, and puzzles and promoted values such as frugality and hard work (much like Franklin's *Poor Richard's Almanack*). Even though the magazine was educational in nature, Child found ways to skew the magazine toward more controversial topics such as racial equality, aiming to inculcate a sense of acceptance into her young readers' minds.

Pioneer Cookbooks

Cookbooks that emphasized thrift and frugality were popular during the pioneer era. The books were usually small in size to accommodate families traveling westward.

Child next turned her attention to women and the household, writing *The Frugal Housewife, Dedicated to Those Who Are Not Ashamed of Economy* (1829). The book was ostensibly a pioneer cookbook containing household tips, recipes, and practical information on buying and storing food, but its emphasis on the virtue of self-reliance marked Child's attempt to elevate the status of domesticity and "middle up" the lower class of women who couldn't afford servants.

In 1831, Child reached a turning point in her life when she met William Lloyd Garrison, a star leader of the abolitionist movement. With his support, she published *An Appeal in Favor of That Class of Americans Called Africans* (1833), which argued for the immediate emancipation of slaves without compensation to slaveholders, a radical stance at the time. While the book gained her entry into the elite abolitionist circle in the North, it ostracized her from the general public. The editor of the *North American Review* publicly denounced the book, and subscriptions to Child's magazine *The Juvenile Miscellany* plummeted.

Issues Over Emancipation

Opponents of immediate emancipation worried that releasing slaves all at once would cause an economic collapse. Child tried to ease those fears by showing how emancipation could be practically achieved, without a dramatic impact on the economy.

Bringing Abolition to the Masses

By 1835, Child recovered from the fallout and adjusted to her new reputation outside the mainstream. She resumed her abolitionist writings, enlarging her aim to the task of educating and shifting the general public's perception of the African American, "familiar[izing] the public mind with the idea that colored people are human beings—elevated or degraded by the same circumstances that elevate or degrade other men."

In 1841, she became the editor of the abolitionist newspaper *National Anti-Slavery Standard* and managed to turn the magazine from a dry, scholarly vehicle of thought to a family newspaper. Circulation of the paper increased dramatically, even rivaling the circulation of the *Liberator,* William Lloyd Garrison's premier abolitionist newspaper. Child had succeeded in bringing the issue of slavery into households and converting many people to the abolitionist cause.

"AND A TWO-FOLD DAMNATION TO YOU, MRS. CHILD!"

Child's fame as an abolitionist writer reached a sensational pinnacle when she published her most famous anti-slavery tract, *Correspondence Between Lydia Maria Child and Gov. Wise and Mrs. Mason, of Virginia* (1860). Over 300,000 copies of the pamphlet were distributed to households across the North and South.

The pamphlet documented a very public argument between Child and the Virginia governor and his wife over the issue of John Brown's famous raid on Harpers Ferry in 1859. It underscored key arguments between the North and South over the issue of slavery, which was now reaching a boiling point.

Mrs. Mason denounced Child in her letters, declaring Child would suffer "two-fold damnation" for supporting such "offscourings of the earth" as John Brown. Child replied that the abolitionists were drawing their attacks from Southern sources, and that knowing what the laws in the slave states advocated should "inspire abhorrence in any humane heart or reflecting mind not perverted by the prejudices of education and custom." Child appealed to a sense of reason and human moral outrage over slavery, and she certainly didn't want to see any Southerners die over the issue of slavery.

Fighter for *All* (Like Douglass)

For the rest of her life, Child continued to devote herself to human rights issues. She published a book called *Incidents in the Life of a Slave Girl* in 1860 based on transcriptions she took of a former slave's account of her life. The book was later recognized as one of the first major autobiographies of a black woman. She wrote a history of societies from biblical times to the nineteenth century that documented what happens in societies where women are respected. Her writings on Native American rights led to the founding of the U.S. Board of Indian Commissioners in 1869. Like Frederick Douglass, Child's chief interest was furthering the rights and equality of *all* people—regardless of race, gender, or class.

WALT WHITMAN

Bard of Democracy

We close this chapter on America's ascent to literary greatness with its crowning achievement, America's first real poet, the "bard of democracy," Walt Whitman (1819–1892).

In his essay "The Poet," Ralph Waldo Emerson describes what an ideal poet looks like and what the poet achieves for his culture and age. After laying it all out in glorious detail, he turns to the reader and says:

> I look in vain for the poet whom I describe. . . . Time and nature yield us many gifts, but not yet the timely man, the new religion, the reconciler, whom all things await. . . . We have yet had no genius in America, with tyrannous eye, which knew the value of our incomparable materials, and saw, in the barbarism and materialism of the times, another carnival of the same gods whose picture he so much admires in Homer; . . . America is a poem in our eyes; its ample geography dazzles the imagination, and it will not wait long for metres.

Emerson was right. America did not have to wait long for its golden "metres"—within ten years of the publication of this essay, Walt Whitman stormed onto the literary scene, publishing his landmark collection of poetry—fresh with new "metres"—called *Leaves of Grass*.

A NEW AMERICAN POETRY

With *Leaves of Grass*, America finally had a poetry that could express the American experience in both *form* and *content*. While

Longfellow wrote about American subjects, he used *traditional* poetic forms and structures that, yes, delighted readers but didn't seem to fully capture the American voice. Whitman's poetry dug deep—it was raw, spoke of the "barbarism and material" of the times, and spoke with a fresh new voice, a "barbaric yawp."

New Poetic Forms

Whitman broke free from almost all of the literary constraints of his time: He ignored traditional forms such as the ballad, he avoided rhyme, and he thumbed his nose at conventional themes and subjects. He wrote poetry in a completely new form called "free verse," which used long lines, rhythms that followed natural speech, and the vocabulary you would hear on any street. His poetry didn't have a regular beat, or rhyme. In fact, there was not much that was "regular" about his poetry at all—even its layout on the page was confusing to readers.

At first, no one liked Whitman's poetry. Literary giants of the establishment such as Longfellow, John Greenleaf Whittier, and the eminent critic James Russell Lowell considered the poetry to be drivel. One person in particular, however, took notice of Whitman's genius, calling it "the most extraordinary piece of wit and wisdom America has yet to contribute." Can you guess who it was? (That would be Ralph Waldo Emerson, of course.)

Barbaric and Explicit

Emerson recognized that Whitman was creating a poetry that married form and content in a way that was fresh and new and could voice the times. But Whitman's poetry was so shocking and new that even Emerson had some trouble with it. Sections of Whitman's poems were overtly sexual, praising the ecstatic, natural joy that comes from the merging of man and woman. His poem "I Sing the Body Electric" describes the "Hair, bosom, hips, bend of legs, negligent falling hands all diffused, mine too diffused" of the poet and a woman in sexual embrace. This didn't sit well with a still very Puritanical America.

What did this exciting poetry look like? Here's a sample from "Song of Myself," from *Leaves of Grass* and Whitman's famous announcement of himself, the poet:

> I celebrate myself, and sing myself,
> And what I assume you shall assume,
> For every atom belonging to me as good belongs to you.
>
> I loafe and invite my soul,
> I lean and loafe at my ease observing a spear of summer grass.
> –(1891–92 version)

You can see how the poetry has no regular line length and seems to flow across the page; the phrasing of the poetry is as long as the phrase of poetic thought. The poet is not aiming to impress anyone with precise meters and rhymes—this is a poet celebrating the joys of the soul connecting with nature.

Transcendental Poet

Think of how Emerson would have recognized the philosophy of transcendentalism in these lines:

> You shall no longer take things at second or third hand,
>> nor look through the eyes of the dead,
>> nor feed on the spectres in books,
> You shall not look through my eyes either, nor take things from me,
> You shall listen to all sides and filter them from your self.

Top: A replica of the *Mayflower* docked in Plymouth Harbor reminds visitors of the Plymouth Colony, one of the early settlements of Europeans in America, which began the creation of an American literature.

Bottom: Thomas Jefferson drafted the Declaration of Independence, influenced by the ideas of such Enlightenment sages as John Locke. Here the delegates sign the declaration in July 1776.

Top left: Abigail Adams's letters to and from her husband, John, reveal one of the great intellectual and romantic partnerships in American literature. In a letter, when he was attending the Continental Congress, she admonished him, "Remember the ladies." **Top right:** In "Paul Revere's Ride," Henry Wadsworth Longfellow succeeded in mirroring the rhythm of a galloping horse—as well as creating an American icon. **Bottom:** In 1845, Henry David Thoreau built a small cabin on the shores of Walden Pond in Massachusetts and settled down to observe and live with nature. The literary result, *Walden*, has influenced generations of environmentalists.

Nathaniel Hawthorne's works, such as *The House of the Seven Gables* and *The Scarlet Letter*, reflected America's tortured relationship with its Puritanical past. Hawthorne himself was ashamed of one of his ancestors who had presided over the Salem witch trials.

Thoreau's writings were an expression of American transcendentalism.

Top: The burial site of Edgar Allan Poe depicts a raven to remind visitors of his most famous literary creation. Poe was one of the first voices of American gothic literature.

Bottom: Harriet Beecher Stowe, in her novel *Uncle Tom's Cabin*, enraged Northerners over the evils of slavery. Although the novel was criticized as overly sentimental, it was wildly popular in the years leading up to the Civil War.

Frederick Douglass, born to slavery, thundered against it in speeches and in his autobiography, *Narrative of the Life of Frederick Douglass, an American Slave, Written by Himself*. He became the voice of the abolitionist movement before the outbreak of the Civil War.

Photo credit: Getty Images/wynnter

No poet, perhaps, more embodies the notion of an American literary voice than Walt Whitman. His *Leaves of Grass* broke new ground poetically while celebrating the exuberance of the growing country.

Photo credit: Getty Images/wynnter

Top left: An illustration by E.W. Kemble from the original 1884 edition of Mark Twain's *The Adventures of Huckleberry Finn.*

Top right: Mark Twain, who took his pen name from a term used while he was a steamboat pilot on the Mississippi River, became the nineteenth century's foremost American humorist.

Bottom: In the 1920s, "flappers," young women wearing fringed dresses and smoking cigarettes, danced to jazz music in New York nightclubs. F. Scott Fitzgerald's *The Great Gatsby* is set in this vibrant scene.

Top: During the 1930s, dust storms swept over the Midwest, driving small farmers off the land and impelling them to go west in search of a better life.

Bottom: John Steinbeck rose to fame on the strength of his 1939 novel *The Grapes of Wrath*, which featured a Dust Bowl farming family, the Joads. His broader subject was the American underclass in the early twentieth century.

Robert Frost's poetry, such as his well-loved "Stopping by Woods on a Snowy Evening," reflected the stark tones and rhythms of his beloved New England.

Whitman, the Original "Hippie"

Whitman's life was as free and irregular as the style of his poetry. He was born in West Hills, on Long Island, and spent much of his life in Brooklyn. By age eleven he was out in the workforce and held a number of odd jobs throughout his teens and his twenties, ranging from schoolteacher to journalist. These brought him in touch with people from all walks of life. His opinionated and radical views and distaste for working often got him fired from jobs. Whitman eventually moved back home to Brooklyn in his thirties to care for his sick father, and it was during this time he began writing *Leaves of Grass*. He lived in cramped quarters in the attic, even at one point sharing a bed with his brother.

WHITMAN, BARD OF DEMOCRACY

Whitman poured his experiences into his poetry, which earned him the title the "bard of democracy." The poet identified himself with the fireman ("I am the mashed fireman with breast-bone broken.... I heard the yelling shouts of my comrades."), "the hounded slave" ("I am the hounded slave, I wince at the bite of the dogs."), and other people who made up the American landscape in the mid-nineteenth century. He expressed myriad voices using the sights, sounds, and smells that defined their experiences. His poetry expressed the experiences of the American people at the time.

Whitman's Star Rises

Whitman witnessed some of the greatest changes in America, living until the 1890s, long after the Civil War ended. He mourned Abraham Lincoln's death greatly and grew disappointed with the

America that emerged after the Civil War with the Reconstruction era. Despite his disappointments, an appreciation for his works grew in his final years and people began to see him as an original voice rather than an unsophisticated and distasteful poet. He continued working on *Leaves of Grass* until his death, expanding the number of poems to 300 from the twelve he published in the original edition in 1855. His poems are still popular today.

The Death of Lincoln

Two of Whitman's most famous poems—"When Lilacs Last in the Dooryard Bloom'd" and "O Captain! My Captain!"—were written about Lincoln. Lincoln's death signaled the passing of a great era to Whitman, and he wrote elegiacally of his passing.

EMILY DICKINSON

Recluse in White

Poets tend to be a rebellious lot. If prevailing poetic conventions don't work, the poets will twist, turn, bend, and break words to fit their purpose. If a traditional meter won't capture the music poets hear in their heads, they'll alter it. If a rhyme scheme seems too confining, they'll break it. This is one of the ways language moves forward.

While Whitman was breaking all sorts of conventions while (ironically) living in his parents' home in New York, quiet recluse Emily Dickinson (1830–1886) was doing the same from her home in western Massachusetts. These two writers toiled away in their childhood bedrooms ushering in an entirely new literary era in poetry, like the mad literary hellions they were. Like all writers ahead of their time, no one really knew what to do with them.

That "Disgrace," Whitman

When asked about Whitman's poetry, Dickinson said she heard it was a "disgrace" and that she hadn't read it.

Emily and Walt: Two Eccentrics

Though their names have since been paired together as the poets who ushered in the modernist movement in poetry, Dickinson was no ruffian like Whitman. Dickinson came from a well-respected family in Amherst, Massachusetts, and was given an outstanding education. In her early years, she seemed like any other young woman socially, attending social events, reading clubs, and other normal activities of her class. But by her early thirties, Emily withdrew. She never left her house, saw only her immediate family, and developed a habit of dressing only in white.

Many Written, Few Published

Of the nearly 2,000 poems Dickinson wrote during her lifetime, only seven were published. After a brief and painful foray into the publishing world, Dickinson kept her poems private.

No one knows for sure what happened. Some say Dickinson became heartbroken over a failed love affair (many scholars have tried to discover who the mystery lover could have been—male or female), some say her strong-willed father influenced her to stay home, and others say she realized that in order to fulfill her brilliance and complete her life's work, she would have to give up a "normal" life and work alone (sort of like Thoreau). Whatever the reason, work she did—in her life she produced nearly 2,000 poems.

Dickinson's Iconic Style

Dickinson's style was highly unconventional for the time. Her style was so unconventional that in order to publish it, editors often stripped out its stylistic features and restored the poems to more conventional usages of style and sense. Either they didn't recognize the value of her eccentric style, or they feared the public wouldn't recognize it and would consider her poems rubbish. It took more than 100 years for her poems to see publication in their original state.

Stylistically, Dickinson is most remembered for two things: her dashes and her use of "slant rhyme" or "off-rhyme." Along with her imagery, these features of her poems helped establish modernist poetry in the twentieth century (more on that later).

Hidden Passions

Dickinson was definitely not a squeaky-clean poet: Check out her poem 249. Like the metaphysical poet John Donne (whom she studied), she fused spiritual passion with sexual desire in carefully wrought conceits, or extended metaphors.

Slant rhyme, or off-rhyme, or near-rhyme, or lazy rhyme, or ... (the term has many variants!) is a rhyme in which the sounds are similar but not identical. Take Dickinson's poem 465:

I heard a Fly buzz—when I died—
The Stillness in the Room
Was like the Stillness in the Air—
Between the Heaves of Storm—

In these lines, *Room/Storm* is an example of slant rhyme. The words sound similar, but the vowel sounds are definitely off. The words even look as if they *ought* to rhyme. By using slant rhyme, Dickinson freed herself to more possibilities with rhyme.

With slant rhyme she also created a sense of dissonance from the ballad form, on which many of her poems are based. People were used to hearing that perfect *abab* rhyme scheme, which writers such as Longfellow used.

Dickinson's use of dashes was also highly unusual and idiosyncratic. Many of her poems end with dashes, which was unusual at the time. In fact, when her longtime confidant and editor published her poems after her death, he "cleaned them up" by adding titles, improving rhymes, and restoring traditional punctuation. This is not what Dickinson intended. Consider what happened when her poem 986, a poem about an encounter with a snake, was published. Here's Dickinson's version:

A narrow Fellow in the Grass
Occasionally rides—
You may have met Him—did you not
His notice sudden is—

The edited version read:

A narrow Fellow in the Grass
Occasionally rides—
You may have met Him—did you not
His notice sudden is.

By removing the dash at the end of the poem and replacing it with a period, the meaning of the poem is altered. The sense of suspense created by the dash is gone. The inverted syntax ("His notice sudden is"), which had suggested how uncomfortable the speaker is with this encounter in nature, is now jammed neatly against a period instead of an open dash, and the speaker now seems more relaxed and certain.

Dickinson's poems were also unusual for their time because of her favored choice of theme: death. While other poets certainly wrote about death, they didn't write about it in the stark, unflinching way Dickinson did. Her spare language and forceful, concrete imagery made her approach to the topic highly philosophical and intellectually brave. In her poem 465, she follows the speaker's mind as he or she approaches the moment of his or her death. In characteristic fashion, she ends the poem with a dash:

> With Blue—uncertain stumbling Buzz—
> Between the light—and me—
> And then the Windows failed—and then
> I could not see—

Dickinson's use of the dash at the end of the poem leaves us in suspense (imagine, again, what it would seem like if the poem ended with a period). Dickinson does something else, though; she leaves us with the phrase "I could not see" before the dash: Does this suggest that the body dies with the soul? The fly, a common symbol for Beelzebub, or the Lord of the Flies, would have been very disconcerting to readers of her time. The poem achieves drama and suspense, and presents an unsettling philosophical statement about the nature of death and immortality.

Although it took years for people to fully embrace her work, Dickinson's fame is now firm. Dozens of major writers have since claimed her as inspiration including William Carlos Williams and Robert Frost. Her philosophical tone and theme, concrete imagery, and highly unique use of punctuation and rhyme have helped established her as one of the nineteenth century's foremost poets. She accomplished all of this from a small, private room in Amherst.

Chapter 5

Realism and Naturalism

In the decades after the Civil War, America was faced with the enormous task of rebuilding itself. The Civil War cost the nation more than 600,000 lives—that's more American casualties than in both World Wars, the Korean War, and the Vietnam War combined. After a period of prosperity, the country was now in debt. After a period of idealism, the country was now morally exhausted.

A brighter future was ahead, though. Even though the war was costly, it spurred a burst of technological and economic growth that moved the country forward. The first transcontinental railroad, the mass expansion of electricity into people's homes, and the invention of the telephone connected people in unprecedented ways. Huge deposits of coal, oil, iron, gold, and silver drew people west where they became rich. The country was on its way to becoming the richest nation in the world.

But while the nation was expanding economically, it was retracting spiritually and intellectually. People were beginning to take a hard, cold look at American ideals that drove them to war, especially in the face of disappointing Reconstruction policies that failed to live up to the war's promise of granting blacks equal rights. A new form of literature called realism developed that represented what America *really* looked and sounded like. Writers such as Mark Twain sought to represent matters truthfully, stripped of the pretenses of romanticism.

Moreover, Charles Darwin's new theory of natural selection was radically changing peoples' ideas of their place in nature. The "best of us" may have gotten there by virtue of "survival of the fittest," not by God's "special appointment" as Puritans thought. America was on the verge of a huge industrial explosion, with plenty of opportunities to become rich—and plenty of opportunities to fall into poverty and despair. Thousands of immigrants poured into the nation and into the hungry jaws of robber barons ready to exploit them. As a result, a new field of literature opened up called naturalism. Writers such as Stephen Crane and Jack London looked at humans' relationship to nature and saw beings caught in an indifferent universe. Writers like Henry James and Edith Wharton looked at the individual's relationship to society and saw people caught in an oppressive web. People saw life as having no purpose other than survival; humans were, in many ways, a product of their society and ultimately subject to laws outside of their control.

MARK TWAIN

American Humorist and "Dean of American Literature"

Mark Twain (1835–1910) wasn't born in the Northeast (the literary hub of America in the mid-nineteenth century), didn't come from a wealthy family or have a college degree, and writing wasn't his dream career (being a riverboat captain was). Nevertheless, Twain achieved a level of literary prestige and worldwide celebrity during his lifetime that was nearly unsurpassed at the time. He is still celebrated today as one of America's finest writers and humorists.

Mr. Clemens and Mr. Twain

Mark Twain's real name was Samuel Clemens. He took his pen name from the phrase river boatmen used ("Mark twain!") to signal when a boat had reached water two fathoms (twelve feet) deep, and the boat could safely pass.

Twain grew up in the sleepy river town of Hannibal, Missouri, where he spent much of his time wandering riverbanks and watching steamboats pass. When Twain's father, a justice of the peace, died when Twain was twelve years old, Twain left school to work in order to help keep the family out of abject poverty. His first job was as an apprentice to a printer.

Twain worked for a few years before he got restless and set off across America, hopping from job to job. A trip down the Mississippi River rekindled his boyhood love of steamboats, and Twain offered a steamboat captain $500 to teach him the trade. He spent a number of happy months learning how to navigate the Mississippi River and becoming a certified pilot. A year after becoming a steamboat pilot, Twain got his brother, Henry, a job aboard the vessel. Tragically, his brother died after the boat's boiler exploded.

During his tenure as pilot, Twain was paid very well and finally became financially secure. Unfortunately, the outbreak of the Civil War halted the riverboat business, and Twain once again found himself out of work and on the streets. Twain didn't leave completely empty-handed, though: His experiences as a steamboat pilot on the Mississippi River helped him create his masterpiece—*Adventures of Huckleberry Finn* (1885)—as well as his affectionate memoir of steamboating days, *Life on the Mississippi*.

Huckleberry Finn

"All modern literature comes from one book by Mark Twain called *Huckleberry Finn*," wrote Ernest Hemingway. Now *that's* a big statement. So what exactly did Hemingway mean by it?

Reviewing Himself

One of Twain's first reviewers? Himself. When he published his first book *Innocents Abroad*, he also published a glowing review of the book, anonymously.

Before Twain's *Huckleberry Finn*, no one really thought that a boy from small-town America was dignified enough to be a main character of a novel, much less its narrator. And while the use of common, everyday speech in novels wasn't unheard of (Harriet Beecher Stowe used the vernacular in *Uncle Tom's Cabin*), it wasn't used all the way through as Twain used it in *Huckleberry Finn*. Also, unlike famous writers such as Stowe, Twain didn't soften his characters with sentimentality: He presented them with all of their prejudices, coarse language, and racist tendencies intact. In these ways, Twain helped usher in the realism movement in American literature and created a new national voice.

TWAIN'S STYLE

Twain's writing is very distinct. You can usually get a sense of his style in just a short passage. Take, for example, the first page of *Adventures of Huckleberry Finn*, where the title character, Huckleberry Finn, introduces himself to the reader:

> You don't know about me without you have read a book by the name of *The Adventures of Tom Sawyer*; but that ain't no matter. That book was made by Mr. Mark Twain, and he told the truth, mainly. There was things which he stretched, but mainly he told the truth.

In this passage, we hear the voice of a poor boy out of the pre-Civil War Mississippi River valley—not your typical main character in a nineteenth-century novel. We also catch our first glimpses of Twain's trademark satire: Twain uses Huckleberry Finn's voice to wryly make a statement about the literary aims of realism—to tell the truth without romantic flourish. It's all in there in one small paragraph.

In general, Twain's style carried these distinctive features:

- The use of vernacular, or regional dialect, of "real" people, usually those found in the outskirts of America

- An unlikely hero—in the case of *Huckleberry Finn*, a poor boy from the South
- Satire that exposed social and religious hypocrisy emerging in America after the Civil War

Realism

Realism was a major literary movement in America in the late nineteenth century. As a rejection of romanticism, it presented the details of ordinary life in art—even the unsavory ones—in an effort "to tell the truth." Supernatural elements found in gothic literature such as Edgar Allan Poe's writings were left behind. The movement gave rise to regionalism in literature, where certain attributes like dialect, attitudes, and beliefs of a certain area were given significance in art. It also gave rise to naturalism, which examined the destructive forces of nature at play in a rising industrial economy that preyed on the weak and squashed an individual's free will.

Huck's and Jim's Adventures

Adventures of Huckleberry Finn follows the story of Huck and his adventures in the company of an escaped slave named Jim. Huck and Jim meet on an abandoned island, and both are seeking refuge—Huck from his abusive father, and Jim from his slave owner, who wants to sell him. At first, Huck is uncomfortable planning an escape down the river with a fugitive slave, but he agrees to keep Jim's secret. Their plan is to raft down the river and catch a steamboat and head to Illinois, a free state.

Along the way Huck and Jim are involved in a bloody feud between two warring Southern families and become prey to two con men pretending to be royalty, the Dauphin and the duke. After a number of mix-ups and failures, Huck and Jim find themselves way off course and further into slave territory, where Huck's conscience is tested. Jim has been sold out by the duke and the Dauphin, who've collected the reward money offered for the capture of a runaway slave. Huck's companion is now imprisoned by a local family while they wait for his true owner to make an appearance.

Typewriting First

Mark Twain was one of the first writers to use a typewriter to compose his works. However, later in life he invested—and lost—a great deal of money in an automatic typesetting machine.

Huck experiences a crisis over whether to abandon Jim or not. In the beginning of the novel, the Widow Douglas, who took Huck in, and her sister tried to "sivilize" Huck by teaching him about morality and religion. Now confused about what the "right" thing to do is, Huck begins to write a letter to Jim's owner revealing her runaway slave's whereabouts. However, remembering all of the things Jim has done to help him during their adventures, he decides not to send it:

It was a close place. I took it up, and held it in my hand. I was a trembling, because I'd got to decide, forever, betwixt two things, and I knowed it. I studied a minute, sort of holding my breath, and then says to myself: "All right, then, I'll go to hell"—and tore it up.

In creating this "crisis" of conscience, Twain is actually revealing the hypocrisy of religious institutions and their slavish followers. In being "bad," Huck is actually "good"—he's clearly more humane than the sanctimonious women who tried to "sivilize" him in the beginning. By exposing this deeply embedded hypocrisy in American culture, Twain offered an alternative to the American "success story." True success could be found in the wilderness, away from the corrupting influence of society.

"It is better to keep your mouth shut and appear stupid than to open it and remove all doubt."

—Mark Twain

Twain's Late Life and Legacy

In total, Twain wrote more than fifteen major works, including a collection of his famous humor writings and a history of his personal hero, Joan of Arc (he considered this book his best). He became internationally recognized for his writings and humor, and in his later years was honored with degrees from Oxford and Yale. His legacy still endures today: In 1998, one of the most prestigious awards in humor was established in his name. People such as Richard Pryor, Steve Martin, Whoopi Goldberg, and Tina Fey have won the Mark Twain Prize for American Humor.

EDITH WHARTON AND HENRY JAMES

The Literary Upper Crust

If you've ever wondered what it was like to be rich and famous in the Victorian era, look no further than Edith Wharton (1862–1937) and Henry James (1843–1916), our official literary guides to the lifestyles of the (nineteenth century's) rich and famous.

Wharton came from the wealthiest of wealthy: The term "keeping up with the Joneses" is based on Wharton's aunt Mary Mason Jones and her lavish Fifth Avenue apartment in New York City.

James came from a distinguished family of academics (his brother, William James, was a leading philosopher and psychologist). Both of these authors used literary realism to penetrate the darker sides of the social and political structures that began to emerge after the Civil War.

Wharton and James were part of the Gilded Age, a period in the late nineteenth century when rapid economic growth gave rise to a newly wealthy class, one that often lacked the social graces and virtues that came with such a position. Mark Twain coined the term in his 1873 novel, *The Gilded Age: A Tale of Today*, in which he satirized the corruptness of the era hidden under a thin veneer of social pretense. Corrupt businessmen, unscrupulous speculators, and scandalous politicians often took advantage of the lack of regulations that came with rapid expansion. The term "gilded" refers to the practice of wrapping a thin layer of gold over an object.

Henry James's father was a well-known intellectual and philosopher who believed in Swedenborgianism, a religious movement founded by Emanuel Swedenborg, who believed God had given him a series of revelations about the Second Coming of Christ. Wharton's parents were real estate, banking, and shipping tycoons. Both James and Wharton had excellent educations and spent much of their youth in Europe, which was common for people of their class.

This experience could be jarring. Despite their European experiences, James and Wharton were still Americans, and American culture and European culture were very different. Wharton, upon returning to America, said she and her other American friends are "wretched exotics produced in a European glass-house," stuck between "the old & the new, . . . the stored beauty & tradition & amenity over there, & the crassness here."

Wharton and James moved in the same intellectual circles and met in the late 1880s. He was already a famous author, and she was just beginning to rise in fame. They didn't become close until Wharton asked James for his opinion of her work. He was harsh but honest, which won her trust and loyalty. They shared a long, fruitful friendship.

HENRY JAMES'S NOVELS

Henry James's novels document the changing, complex relationship between the Old World and the New as a wealthy class was born in America. Employing a new type of realism called *psychological realism*, James explored the underpinnings of American and European values through a psychological exploration of his characters and a realistic depiction of their experiences. As a result, his writing style could become complex, convoluted, and difficult to read (probably why people more often *say* they've read his books than actually have—they're hard!).

In his novella *Daisy Miller*, James explores the Old World and the New World through the psychology of the title character, Daisy Miller. Daisy is a young woman in her prime who travels to Europe. Unaware of how a "proper lady" should act during dating, she makes several fatal blunders that cost her the hand of her handsome, sophisticated European suitor. Daisy's naivety is a commentary on American culture's inability to compete with the prejudices of European culture.

In another famous novel, *The Portrait of a Lady* (1881), James writes about a young American woman who suddenly comes into money and quickly becomes a target for schemers. Once again, the Old and New World clash, and James's characters struggle to find their moral centers in the shifting codes of the times.

EDITH WHARTON

Wharton had her own brand of realism that also exposed the problems that America faced as the Old World clashed with the New. Acutely aware of the stifling circumstances a woman in her class faced, Wharton wrote complex novels that showed characters in confining social obligations that threatened their individual freedom. Wharton cast a keen eye on the moral "blindness" and corruption of her class.

In her novel *The House of Mirth* (1905), Wharton tells the story of Lily Bart, a twenty-nine-year-old woman born into all the right circumstances but with all the wrong luck. Having lost her wealth, she struggles to regain her position in society. Lily is a complex personality, torn between a desire to regain her position and an inability to go against her inner longing for what she feels is "right." She ends up ruined, done in by her failure to fully play by society's rules.

In her novel *The Age of Innocence* (1920), Wharton writes about an upper-class man who is thwarted at every turn by taboos to marry a woman he suddenly finds himself in love with. She's the exact opposite of the perfect, boring social flower he is engaged to marry. Ultimately he fails to marry the woman he truly loves and has to resign himself to his circumstances. Wharton wrote the novel when she was well into her fifties, after she had witnessed how World War I shattered people's dreams and left them with a new reality. In many ways, the man's loss of love reflects the loss of the American dream after the war.

Novel of Manners

Wharton's novels belong to a subgenre of realism called *novels of manners*. These give rich descriptions of social worlds in which characters are quietly measured against how well they behave against social norms. Like Huck in Mark Twain's *Adventures of Huckleberry Finn*, characters who behave outside of social norms are perceived as being "wrong" when they are actually "right." The English writer Jane Austen also wrote novels of manners—her popular novels like *Pride and Prejudice* used comedy and a lighter tone to expose flaws in nineteenth-century English society.

Like other writers of realism, Wharton had a fine eye for detail. Her novels were full of vivid, rich descriptions of places such as Victorian sitting rooms, perfectly plumped couch cushions, and the richly dressed (and bored) women who sat on them. On the surface, her novels satisfied people's natural curiosity about the lifestyles of the rich and famous.

Underneath all of these realistic portrayals of the upper class, however, Wharton layered her sharp satiric wit, which made her the masterful, celebrated writer she was. By focusing on details, she could present herself as a detached observer of upper-class life while quietly satirizing it. In this way, she was a writer of naturalism, since she took a scientific approach to her analysis of the mechanisms of society. Her novels exposed the ways in which upper-class society's codes restricted a person's individuality and free will.

A Late but Great Start

Wharton gave conventional marriage a solid try, but after a decade of marriage she was mentally exhausted, on the verge of a nervous breakdown, trying to keep up the pretense of being married to a man she didn't love. As a member of the social elite, she was expected to be a mute ornament to her husband, not a writer. Family, friends, and social peers discouraged her writing ambition.

As a result, Wharton didn't publish her first book until she was thirty-six years old. She may have had a late start, but she published fifty books in nearly forty years. In 1921, she became the first woman to win the Pulitzer Prize, which was awarded for her novel *The Age of Innocence* (her twelfth novel). In all, she was nominated for the Nobel Prize in Literature three times.

KATE CHOPIN AND CHARLOTTE PERKINS GILMAN

Early Feminists

"Whatever have been the cares of the day, greet your husband with a smile when he returns. Make your personal appearance just as beautiful as possible. Let him enter rooms so attractive and sunny that all the recollections of his home, when away from the same, shall attract him back."

—*Hill's Manual of Social and Business Forms*, 1888

In the late nineteenth century, the role of women began to change. Before, women's chief roles were as a wife and mother. Their job was to maintain the home, uphold their children's education, and support their husbands, especially by helping to uphold his role in society. Women were the spiritual and moral center of the household.

But times were changing. Women could now find work in factories and earn money on their own. Social reform movements such as abolitionism saw women at the podium as well as men. Women could now take more active roles in public affairs. Divorce laws began to loosen, allowing women greater rights to make divorce claims and gain custody of their children. Before, men were automatically granted sole custody of the children after a divorce. As the country became more industrialized and socially progressive, there were greater roles for women outside the home, and newer ways for them to define themselves.

Resistance to Change

Women's roles as wives and mothers were considered so sacred and essential to the nation that when these roles began to change there was a feeling that the very fabric of the nation itself was being threatened.

Tension increased as women struggled to navigate their place in the face of these new opportunities. How could a woman best serve her family, husband, and country? The pressures women faced were captured in two important works of the era: "The Yellow Wallpaper" by Charlotte Perkins Gilman and *The Awakening* by Kate Chopin.

CHARLOTTE PERKINS GILMAN

Charlotte Perkins Gilman (1860–1935) was a controversial person both in her personal life and in her writing. Her great aunt was none other than Harriet Beecher Stowe, another strong and controversial female figure of the nineteenth century.

When Gilman was still an infant, her father walked out on her family. Her mother responded in a strange way: Determined to toughen Charlotte up, she withheld affection from her as a child. She felt this was a way to protect Charlotte from the disillusionment she experienced in her own life.

Of course, this deeply scarred Gilman who characterized her childhood as "painful and lonely." Gilman determined never to marry, probably to protect herself. When she met the attractive young artist Charles Walter Stetson, however, she changed her mind. They married when she was twenty-four years old. Bad from the start, the marriage failed after Charlotte fell into a deep postpartum depression when their daughter Katherine was born.

Charlotte was convinced that her marriage was stifling her and causing her depression. She divorced Stetson in an attempt to save her sanity. Stetson quickly remarried, and in another bold move, Charlotte sent their daughter to live with them. She herself became a social pariah.

During the nineteenth century, a popular method of treating women's depression such as Gilman's was to prescribe a "rest cure." A rest cure consisted of acting as "domestic as possible," to not touch "pen, pencil, or brush," and commit to only two hours of mental exertion a day. (Now *that* was enough to make anyone insane.)

Of course, Gilman was suspicious of this highly regarded cure. She wrote a story, "The Yellow Wallpaper" (1892), to recount the disastrous effects rest cures had on women. People were outraged with the portrayal and claimed the story would make women crazy. Gilman defended herself in her essay, "Why I Wrote The Yellow Wallpaper," claiming, "It was not intended to drive people crazy, but to save people from being driven crazy, and it worked." In its time, though, people were unable (or refused) to see the story as a critique of society. They read it as an unfortunate tale about a crazy woman.

In scenes reminiscent of Poe's "The Tell-Tale Heart," the story follows the slow deterioration of a woman's mind. Her well-meaning husband locks her away in a room so she can recover from her depression. With nothing to do, the woman stares at the room's yellow wallpaper. She begins hallucinating, seeing a woman crawling and creeping about the patterns, which she interprets as "bars."

Finally, the narrator completely loses her mind. Her husband finds her in the room ripping the wallpaper off the walls and walking around in circles. She keeps her shoulder against the wall so "she doesn't lose her way." The woman now identifies herself with the woman in the wallpaper. When her husband asks her what she is doing, she explains,

> I've got out at last . . . in spite of you and Jane. And I've pulled off most of the paper, so you can't put me back!

Horrified, her husband faints, and the woman continues pacing around the room, walking over his body each time around.

KATE CHOPIN

Kate Chopin (1851–1904) was born in St. Louis, Missouri. At age nineteen, she married a young cotton broker named Oscar Chopin and moved to New Orleans with him. They had a happy union that lasted twelve years. Unfortunately, Oscar died in 1882 and Chopin had to provide for herself and their children.

Chopin began writing to earn money. She was successful and earned a reputation as a writer of regional fiction of the South. When she published her novel *The Awakening* in 1899, Chopin lost her success. Although the book was praised for its craft, Chopin's depiction of a woman protagonist who was sexually aware and determined to find her own identity outside of being a wife and mother was shocking for the time. The book was condemned and banned in libraries.

The Awakening

The Awakening takes place in Louisiana at the end of the nineteenth century. The novel's protagonist, Edna Pontellier, is in a relatively happy marriage with a successful husband, and has loving, attractive children. She cares for her family, but they don't fulfill her sense of identity. She says, "I would give up the unessential; I would give my money, I would give my life for my children; but I wouldn't give myself." To Chopin's readers, the idea that a mother would not be completely satisfied by her roles as a wife and mother was almost sacrilegious.

Edna says she misses her children while she is away from them, but she reflects that she cares for them in an "uneven, impulsive way." On a serene summer vacation with her family she "awakens" to the fact that she loves her family, but she does not live solely for them.

Encouraged by the independent Mademoiselle Reisz, whose beautiful piano music stirs Edna's awakening, she takes a lover. Unfortunately, things don't work out. Edna decides that the only way to full self-realization is by committing suicide. She follows the "seductive" voice of the sea, "inviting the soul to wander in abysses of solitude." As she is swimming further out in the ocean, her arms and legs growing tired, she thinks of her husband and children: "They were a part of her life. But they need not have thought that they could possess her, body and soul."

Both Chopin and Gilman are considered naturalist writers since they framed their characters as being "fated," their fates ultimately determined by the framework of society (more on naturalists in the next section). For Chopin, Edna Pontellier's final act of suicide can be read as a heroic, positive act of affirmation—she would rather leave life on her own terms than resign herself to the emotional dead end that society can only offer her as a woman. For Gilman, the message is the same, if a little more bleakly presented—the only way women can be accepted into society is if they are emptied of their psychological, emotional, and spiritual vitality. In society's attempts to "heal" Gilman's protagonist, she has become its living, yet psychologically devoid, victim.

STEPHEN CRANE AND JACK LONDON

Voices of the People

"When it occurs to a man that nature does not regard him as important, and that she feels she would not maim the universe by disposing of him, he at first wishes to throw bricks at the temple, and he hates deeply the fact that there are no bricks and no temples. Any visible expression of nature would surely be pelleted with his jeers."

—Stephen Crane, "The Open Boat"

STEPHEN CRANE:
LIVE FAST, DIE YOUNG

Stephen Crane (1871–1900) was the kind of person you might find at a seedy bar well past last call. Crane befriended prostitutes, chain-smoked, and became a fixture of the 1890s Bowery district scene in New York. In his lifetime, he survived a shipwreck, sailed to Greece, mingled with famous writers, inspired writers generations older than him, and established a new field of literature. He did this all in the short twenty-eight years he was alive.

Crane was born in Newark, New Jersey, in 1871. He was the youngest of fourteen children. His father was a preacher and wanted Crane to follow in his career. Crane enrolled in a seminary and lasted for two years. After a few more attempts at making a go of college in New York and Pennsylvania, he landed a position with the *New York Tribune* as a reporter.

In New York Crane came face-to-face with the darker sides of life. He became a regular customer of the Tenderloin hookers and developed a sensitivity to their condition. At twenty he proposed to a married woman but ended up marrying the madam of a well-known brothel, Cora Taylor.

The Life of Man Is Nasty, Brutal, and Short

Crane used his experiences in the Bowery to write his first novel, *Maggie: A Girl of the Streets* (1893). Maggie comes from a rough background—her parents are alcoholics and Maggie witnesses her parents' physical and emotional abuse. Vulnerable, she falls prey to a barkeep named Pete who loves her and leaves her. Her parents judge Maggie a disgrace and kick her out. Homeless, she turns to prostitution. Only after she dies do the people close to her recognize that she was a good girl reduced by her circumstances.

The novel caught the attention of William Dean Howells, an important literary critic at the time who recognized Crane's talent. Two years later, Crane wrote the novel he is most famous for, *The Red Badge of Courage* (1895). Though Crane never served in any war, his portrayal of the psychological effects of war were remarkably realistic. The novel tells the tale of the Civil War from the point of view of a soldier.

In 1897, Crane became involved in Cuba's war for independence from Spain and set sail for the island on a ship carrying ammunition for Cuba's revolutionaries. The ship sank and Crane found himself adrift at sea with three other men in a dinghy for thirty hours before landing in Florida. The experience became the basis for another one of Crane's masterpieces, the short story "The Open Boat."

Humans: Nature's Playthings

"The Open Boat," more than any other of Crane's works, became a keystone work of naturalism, a new literary movement begun by the French writer Émile Zola. Naturalism examined the effects heredity, environment, and chance had on the course of a human's life. Naturalists often painted very bleak pictures in their novels—pictures where people were determined by their circumstances and had very little control over their lives. Like realist writers, naturalist writers sought to represent life as truthfully as possible. Naturalism was a more negative offshoot of realism, as dark romanticism was to transcendentalism (there are always two sides to one coin).

Émile Zola

Émile Zola's twenty-volume series Les Rougon-Macquart, published between 1871 and 1893, is considered one of the landmark works of naturalism. The novels demonstrate a key feature of naturalism in literature: the application of the scientific method to characters, recording their conditions, heredity, environment, and behavior in a detached, objective way.

A Cold, Indifferent Universe

"The Open Boat" (1897) opens with four men adrift at sea in a boat: an oiler, a cook, the captain, and the narrator. The men face a merciless, indifferent sea:

> None of them knew the color of the sky. Their eyes glanced level, and were fastened upon the waves that swept toward them. These waves were of the hue of slate, save for the tops, which were of foaming white. . . . The horizon narrowed and widened, and

dipped and rose, and at all times its edge was jagged with waves that seemed thrust up in points like rocks.

The men finally spot shore and they make a mad dash for it. Only three of the men survive the rough surf. The sea, whether rocky, calm, cruel, or kind, is ultimately indifferent to the concerns of the men. This conflict between humanity and nature underscored a key feature of naturalism: Survival is a matter of chance, and humanity's struggles are, in many ways, futile.

Jack London and His Call to the Wild

Stephen Crane opened the field of naturalism in America; Jack London (1876–1916) gave it a twist. His most famous novel, *The Call of the Wild* (1903), explored naturalism from the perspective of an unlikely character: a dog.

Like Crane, London also had a brush with life's underbelly. As a teenager he jumped from job to job—pirating oysters, working on sealing ships, and joining a fish patrol—and got a firsthand look at the exploitation, poor working conditions, and hardships the nation's workers faced. At one point he discovered socialism and began giving speeches on street corners, earning the title the "boy Socialist of Oakland."

In the 1890s, London began a steady discipline of writing 1,000 words a day. Desperate to escape his fate of a life of drudgery, he felt that writing was his only way out. London began publishing stories in 1899, and after more than fifty books he became one of the nation's wealthiest and most successful writers.

London's novel *The Call of the Wild* finally brought him fame in 1903. The novel is set during the Klondike gold rush of 1896. London was one of the many prospectors who flocked there in 1897. He got a firsthand look at the brutish fight for survival during his experience and used it to shape his novel.

Law of Club and Fang

The novel follows a domesticated dog named Buck who is "jerked from the heart of civilization and flung into the heart of things primordial" after he is stolen from a ranch in California and sold as a sled dog in Alaska. Buck must revert to his "wolf" state and learn the "law of club and fang" now that he is in the wilderness. The novel became a literary example of the survival of the fittest.

Anthropomorphism

Anthropomorphism is a literary device through which an author gives human characteristics to animals or nonliving objects. Anthropomorphism allows authors to explore sensitive social issues in a nonthreatening way. A famous example is George Orwell's *Animal Farm,* published in 1945. Orwell used the device to satirize Stalin and make a statement about the dangers of dictatorship.

Naturalism in literature still exists today, though it has been tempered over the years. Though the philosophical stance of naturalists is largely pessimistic, its ultimate goal was to improve the human condition by exposing it.

Chapter 6

Modernism

After a period of massive expansion in the second half of the nineteenth century, America found itself at the threshold of another catastrophe: a world war. In four short, brutal years from 1914 to 1918, World War I completely changed the world. America had gone from an isolated political player in the world to a country unsure of how to proceed on the world's stage.

The shifting times left people feeling uncertain, spiritually and emotionally. For the soldiers coming home from the war, dealing with reality became a problem—what were they returning to? The traditions and beliefs that used to support them now felt empty and meaningless.

Literature responded by breaking with tradition. In a burst of creativity, writers began experimenting with new forms to capture the feeling of rootlessness and loss of belief that dominated the age. Traditional forms now seemed incapable of expressing the mood of this new age. The poet Ezra Pound called for writers to "make it new," while T.S. Eliot published landmark works that pretty much set the diction, tone, and literary mood for the new era. With all this creative energy, a new movement in literature called modernism was born.

Interestingly, at the heart of modernism lay a very important irony: While there was excitement to move forward and leave old traditions and beliefs behind, there was also a sense of regret that traditions were lost. As a result, you can see writers creating works that both catapulted literature forward and works that more cautiously tried to re-envision traditions to preserve them in some way. Writers either reveled in the chaos or were anxious to put the pieces back together—while some managed to find humor in it all.

THE LOST GENERATION

The Roaring Twenties

"One generation passeth away, and another generation cometh; but the earth abideth forever. . . . The sun also ariseth, and the sun goeth down, and hasteth to the place where he arose."

—Ecclesiastes

The Lost Generation seemed an appropriate term for the twenty- and thirty-somethings who came of age after the war. Soldiers, witness to so much carnage, now returned home and felt like strangers to their own homes. Young people who didn't go to war were just as disaffected—many of them went to Europe to escape the sense of fragmentation at home (also, the drinking age was lower).

The American expatriate Gertrude Stein (1874–1946) was in many ways the literary "mother hen" of the Lost Generation. She counseled writers, gave them support, and put into motion some of the defining artistic philosophies of the era.

A writer and intellectual herself, Stein left to live in Paris when she was young and stayed there for most of her life (though she never considered herself an expatriate—always an American first). She shared an apartment with her partner, Alice B. Toklas, that became a massive hub for writers, intellectuals, artists, and American expatriates. Pablo Picasso, who painted her portrait, and Ernest Hemingway, who immortalized her term "lost generation" in his novel *The Sun Also Rises*, were some of the stars who crossed Stein's threshold.

Stein even christened the Lost Generation: Supposedly, one day in Paris, Stein overheard her car mechanic tell his young workers, who weren't going fast enough, "you're all a lost generation." For Stein, the term stuck.

Gertrude Stein's Style

Gertrude Stein had a radical writing style that in many ways captured the experimental spirit of the modernist era. Her writing aimed to revolutionize what the very function of a *word* was. To Stein, the idea that a word was a carrier of meaning was too traditional, too "patriarchal." She treated words as "objects."

ERNEST HEMINGWAY

Ernest Hemingway (1899–1961) grew up in Oak Park, Illinois, in a quiet middle-class family. After a brief stint as an ambulance driver in World War I in his twenties, he was one of the young people who found it hard to be home. The serenity of Oak Park seemed false compared to the real drama of war he had just experienced. Hemingway decided to pack his bags with his wife to take a job as a European correspondent for the *Toronto Star*. Shortly after he arrived in Paris, he met Gertrude Stein.

Stein became one of the most influential people in Hemingway's life. When Hemingway showed her his writing, she gave him some important advice he took to heart: "A great deal of description, and not particularly good description. Begin over again and concentrate." With Stein's advice, and the many new friendships with famous writers, artists, and intellectuals he cultivated through Stein, Hemingway began to develop his trademark style.

From Ernestine to Papa

Hemingway's mother wanted a girl so badly that she dressed Ernest in girls' clothing, kept his hair long, and called him "Ernestine." Hemingway more than made up for it: At the height of his celebrity, he was considered to be the one of the most masculine writers of the twentieth century. His famous nickname was "Papa."

"Deceptively Simple"

Hemingway's writing style is legendary in the literary world. It became so influential and pervasive in the writing of the twentieth century that some people don't even see it as a style anymore—just the status quo.

Iceberg Theory

Hemingway had a famous theory about his writing style: the principle of the iceberg. For every iceberg, he explains, "seven-eighths of it [is] underwater for every part it shows. . . . Anything you know you can eliminate . . . only strengthens your iceberg." Hemingway's writing represents the strongest one-eighth of that iceberg. His careful pruning helps poise the reader to understand the thing that isn't being said—the reality behind the words.

Critics have called Hemingway's style things like "deceptively simple," "masculine," and "energetic." His sentences are so sparse, direct, and simple that it seems as if a child wrote them. But they were not—they were written by a master, and they skillfully pack a meaningful punch.

The Sun Also Rises

Hemingway's *The Sun Also Rises* (1926) became the novel of the Lost Generation. Set in the 1920s, the novel follows a group of expatriates as they wander aimlessly through France and Spain. The two main characters, Jake Barnes and Lady Brett Ashley, are in love but unable to consummate their relationship because a war wound has left him impotent, and she is unable to do without:

> "Couldn't we live together, Brett? Couldn't we just live together?"
>
> "I don't think so. I'd just *tromper* you with everybody. You couldn't stand it."
>
> "I stand it now."
>
> "That would be different. It's my fault, Jake. It's the way I'm made."
>
> "Couldn't we go off in the country for a while?"
>
> "It wouldn't be any good. I'll go if you like. But I couldn't live quietly in the country. Not with my own true love."
>
> "I know."
>
> "Isn't it rotten? There isn't any use my telling you I love you."

Hope for the Future

The Sun Also Rises begins with two epigraphs: "You are all a lost generation" (attributed to "Gertrude Stein in conversation"), and the quote from the book of Ecclesiastes found at the beginning of this section. By using both quotes, Hemingway suggests a kind of bleak hope: His generation may be lost, but this is all part of the cyclical nature of the universe. The spirit of a generation will regenerate, just as the Earth regenerates.

Jake and Brett symbolize the dissolution of beliefs and spirit that defined the Lost Generation—even the words "I love you" don't mean anything anymore.

The theme of alienation dominates the novel, but Hemingway also takes a stab at some alternative beliefs and values to support what's left of society. Friendship, loyalty, grace under pressure, and stoicism are often offered as substitutes in Hemingway's novels—the basis of a new, if shaky, foundation. In *The Sun Also Rises*, Hemingway casts the bullfighter as a new hero for the Lost Generation. Jake says, "It is the bullfighter who lives life to the hilt, bringing to his work all his courage, intelligence, discipline, and art."

In the end, despite all of his fame, fortune, and friendships, Hemingway became an isolated man in the years before he died. As he won the Nobel Prize in 1954, he remarked, "Writing, at its best, is a lonely life." He committed suicide in 1961.

The Final Masterpiece

Hemingway made massive contributions to literature. One of his last great masterpieces is *The Old Man and the Sea* (1952). It's the story of an old fisherman's attempt to catch a great marlin. Although he succeeds, sharks, attracted by the scent of blood in the water, surround his boat and devour most of the fish.

THE ROARING TWENTIES

The Jazz Age

Not everything was gloom and doom for the Lost Generation, however. The Roaring Twenties showed that without a sense of tradition, people could also have a lot of . . . fun. Women called "flappers" cut their hair short, wore dazzling clothes, and flaunted a more freethinking, independent spirit in open defiance of social norms. Speakeasies popped up in major cities as Prohibition spurred the creation and sale of illegal alcohol. Charlie Chaplin was the leading figure of the silent silver screen and Duke Ellington was the star of the jazz scene. The Roaring Twenties was full of creativity, nonconformity, and life.

The Crash

All that prosperity didn't last long. The stock market crashed in 1929 and plunged America into a deep economic depression that lasted years.

People also became richer during the Roaring Twenties. Prices and taxes were low so it didn't take much money to be considered "upper class." Many people could have a comfortable existence on very little. It could be an all-around good time if you were young in the 1920s.

F. SCOTT FITZGERALD

The writer F. Scott Fitzgerald (1896–1940) captured all that was *good* about the more exuberant side of the 1920s while not neglecting its darker side. In capturing the spirit of the Roaring Twenties and the Jazz Age, Fitzgerald used a style that was much more showy and luxurious than Hemingway's.

The Great Gatsby

F. Scott Fitzgerald's novel *The Great Gatsby* (1925) defined the twenties. *The Great Gatsby* is a lyrically written tale of glitz, glamour, and enchantment. At its core is the romanticism of the American dream that drove the era. Also at its core is a statement of how that dream, in the end, is empty.

Nick, Tom, Daisy, and Jay Gatsby—the Players

The novel is narrated by Nick Carraway, a Midwesterner who moves to West Egg, Long Island, where his cousin Daisy and her husband Tom live. A mysterious man named Jay Gatsby, who owns a huge mansion next door, intrigues Nick. One night Gatsby throws a huge, elaborate party where things get a little too wild. People get drunk, couples fight, and there is even a car accident. Nick and Gatsby become friends, and he begins to learn the truth behind Gatsby's mysterious exterior.

Nick learns that the reason Gatsby is hanging around is that he is secretly angling to win Daisy back after a love affair they had years earlier. Gatsby pins all of his ideals on their reconciliation—Daisy and their relationship is the center of meaning in his world. Nick, the moral center of the novel, warns Gatsby that the past can't be repeated.

In the end, Gatsby's dreams are dashed and he has to face reality. It becomes painfully clear that Daisy's "vast carelessness" will never allow her to leave Tom. When Daisy is revealed to be a shadow of what Gatsby idealizes her to be, it becomes clear that Gatsby loves a representation of Daisy, not who she really is. In the novel, Gatsby's dreams are the American dream, and Daisy's shallowness and materialism represent the hollowness of the American dream. Beneath all of those smiling, pretty faces at the party is despair.

Fitzgerald's life wasn't too far off from Gatsby's. He and his wife Zelda led one of the most public and glamorous lifestyles of the Jazz Age. (They were the Brad and Angelina of their day, except with a lot more booze and a lot more fighting.) Zelda was a bubbly socialite whom Fitzgerald dubbed "the first flapper," and Fitzgerald was a rich, successful, and handsome author. Their hard-partying, extravagant lifestyle captivated the public. It eventually caught up to them, though—Fitzgerald ended up a drunken hack and Zelda was committed to an asylum. Everyone seemed to have an opinion about what caused the decline of the relationship. People on Fitzgerald's side blamed Zelda, saying she ruined Fitzgerald's talent, and people on Zelda's side said Fitzgerald's carelessness drove her to the asylum. Fitzgerald based his novel *The Beautiful and the Damned* on his ill-fated marriage with Zelda.

Uncertainty and confusion, stability and extravagance, rebellion and conformity: The 1920s was an era of extreme highs and lows. No one really knew where the center was in all of the chaos. Hemingway and Fitzgerald exemplified the polarities of the era: stoic aimlessness and careless exuberance. At the core of both was a call for a more meaningful life.

EZRA POUND AND T.S. ELIOT

Two Giants of Modernism

Ezra Pound (1885–1972) and T.S. Eliot (1888–1965) are the two outstanding figures of modernism: They set the tone, diction, and subject matter for the age, and brought poetry into a new era. Eliot's "The Waste Land" (1922) became one of the most important poems of the age, and Pound's creative contributions to the works of major poets—including William Butler Yeats, Robert Frost, and Eliot—made him the driving force behind modernism. Pound's influence was so great that Eliot dedicated his major work "The Waste Land" to him, calling him *"il miglior fabbro"* (the better craftsman).

Il Miglior Fabbro

Eliot's phrase *il miglior fabbro* is a literary allusion to Dante's "Purgatorio" in which Dante uses the phrase as a tip of the hat to Arnaut Daniel, a master troubadour poet of the twelfth century. Here, Eliot is making the same gesture to Pound.

MAKE IT NEW!

Pound had huge literary ambitions from the start. He wrote that, as a young man, his goal was to "know more about poetry than any man living." It would be hard to argue that he didn't achieve his goal.

"Make it new!"—this was Pound's slogan and call to action to his fellow poets. "Poetry must be as well written as prose," he declared, and "its language must be fine language." He felt romanticism had gone too far with its importance on the individual and emotional excesses, and free verse had become too "floppy." He wanted nothing less than to impose a new order on poetic language.

Muscular Poetry

Pound was no joke: He was a master of jujitsu and not afraid to use his skills on his friends. He gave Robert Frost a demonstration by throwing him over his shoulder in a public restaurant.

These principles led to his development of *imagism*, a literary movement that was short-lived but had a dramatic impact on poets and poetry afterwards. Imagism called for:

- Direct treatment of a subject, no excessive "literaryism"
- No unnecessary language
- Rhythm driven by the "music" of the poem, not by artificially imposed meters

The result was a type of poetry that used ordinary language (not "book words," which could weigh a poem down), concise language (not grammatical inversions), and concentrated images to drive the expression of the poem. Here is a stanza from the poem "Sea Lily," by the poet H.D., who Pound thought wrote some of the best examples of imagist poetry:

Reed,
slashed and torn
but doubly rich—
such great heads as yours

drift upon temple-steps,
but you are shattered
in the wind.

In the poem, all of the emotional content is distilled into one central, driving image: the reed, slashed, torn, and shattered in the wind.

Two Giants Meet

Pound and Eliot met in London in 1914. Eliot was diverted there from studying in Germany after the outbreak of World War I. Pound fled to London to escape the "philistine Americans" after a number of clashes with authority figures at Wabash College in Indiana, where he was teaching. Unbeknownst to Pound, Eliot was already writing poetry that encapsulated a lot of Pound's principles and beliefs. The two became fast friends, and with Pound's encouragement, Eliot began publishing his poetry.

At the time, Eliot was working on his poem "The Love Song of J. Alfred Prufrock," which became a hallmark of modernist poetry. The poem is a dramatic monologue from the point of view of a middle-aged man unable to act or find meaning in life. It famously begins:

Let us go then, you and I,
When the evening is spread out against the sky
Like a patient etherized upon a table;

The inner dramatic monologue of the poem shows a man drowning in indecision and an inability to communicate: "'Do I dare? . . . / That is not what I meant at all. / That is not it, at all.'" The poem encapsulates the sense of alienation and ineffectualness that afflicted modern society and sets the poetic tone for the era.

Pound hit the same tone in his poem "Hugh Selwyn Mauberley," published a few years later:

> For three years, out of key with his time,
> He strove to resuscitate the dead art
> Of poetry; to maintain "the sublime"
> In the old sense. Wrong from the start—

Both Eliot's and Pound's poems used traditional forms such as the dramatic monologue and classical allusions to express the state of modern society, but they used them in fragmentary ways. Their poetry was dense and hard to read, since it seemed to have no central organization and used difficult, obscure allusions many people could not easily interpret. It was for these reasons, though, that it was profoundly effective at expressing the sense of spiritual disenfranchisement and fragmentation of modern society—people were disconnected from their own culture.

"The Waste Land"

When Eliot published "The Waste Land" in 1922, fellow poet William Carlos Williams said it "struck like a sardonic bullet." Poets now flocked to Eliot as their "representative man."

In a literal sense, the title of the poem refers to the battlefields of World War I, a waste land of corpses and destruction. Metaphorically, the title and the poem itself capture the spiritual and emotional waste land that resulted from the war. In the poem, sex does not bear fruit, death does not give way to resurrection, and beliefs are not sustaining. The world is a waste land of futility.

ELIOT AND POUND DIVERGE

In a world with such a loss of belief, what were people to do? As poets, Eliot and Pound had two different solutions. All of religion and tradition may have been blown apart and lying in fragments, but for Eliot, a restoration of spirituality could put together a new order or "whole." Pound, on the other hand, was more content with chaos, accepting the new reality for what it was. He believed in culture more than anything, and a carefully restructured society, not tradition, would be the antidote to modern society's ills.

The two took different paths personally as well. Writing "The Waste Land" cost Eliot his sanity and he was admitted to a sanitarium while writing it. He recovered, however, and converted to Episcopalianism, which restored his faith. At the age of sixty, Eliot won the Nobel Prize in Literature, a crowning achievement to a huge career. Pound, on the other hand, engaged more deeply in political affairs over the years and ended up on trial for treason for delivering fascist radio broadcasts against America in Italy during World War II. Pound was found legally insane, narrowly averting a death sentence, and was sent to a sanitarium. While there, he finished his life's work, the *Cantos*, a work in which people see a man repentant for going astray.

Pound's highly experimental poetic *Cantos* had a profound effect on modern literature, just like Eliot's "The Waste Land." The snippets of classical allusion, foreign literature fragments, and authentic language captured the spiritual despair of the times and anticipated the fragmentary way we receive stories today through film, radio, and television. Pound modeled his *Cantos* on Whitman's *Leaves of Grass*, even though (or maybe because) he felt that Whitman's *Leaves of Grass* demonstrated everything *wrong* in poetry. (Let that one sit for a while!)

WILLIAM FAULKNER

Writer of the South

"I believe that man will not merely endure: he will prevail."

—William Faulkner, Nobel Banquet speech

William Faulkner (1897–1962) was born in New Albany, Mississippi, and was raised in Oxford, Mississippi, a nearby town. Though he never finished high school, he read deeply and widely. From his adolescence, Faulkner was determined to become a writer.

In 1918, Faulkner enlisted in the British Royal Flying Corps, eager to experience the drama of war. Unfortunately for him, World War I ended before he ever got to see any action. With the money he earned from the government for his service, he was able to attend the University of Mississippi. He never finished and left at age twenty-three to pursue a writing career in New York City.

Faulkner spent six months in New York before he gave up and went home. For a while, he worked as a postmaster, but, of course, that didn't last long. Faulkner decided to return to writing, despite the odds and the lack of approval he got in New York. He added a "u" to his original name (Falkner) and declared himself a real writer, capital "W."

FAULKNER FINALLY
MAKES HIS MARK

At first, Faulkner concentrated on writing poetry. His first book, a collection of poems called *The Marble Faun*, sold only fifty copies. Next, he tried fiction. His first novel, *Soldiers' Pay*, published with the help of his friend Sherwood Anderson, was his first big break, establishing him as a legitimate writer. Buoyed by this (rather mild) success, he then began work on what would become his masterpiece, *The Sound and the Fury*.

The book was published in 1929 and is considered a masterpiece of twentieth-century American literature. It's *not* an easy read. (Anyone who tells you otherwise is probably bragging.)

Innovative Writer

The novel was highly experimental for its time. Faulkner plays with almost all the usual features of your run-of-the-mill standard way of telling a story. He experiments with:

- **Narration:** The story is told from four viewpoints/multiple narrators, not a single narrator
- **Chronology:** The story is told out of chronological order (*discontinuous time*)
- **Stream of consciousness:** Some sections are told in *stream of consciousness*, a literary device in which a story is told from *inside* a character's mind; the style tries to mimic the way a mind naturally jumps from thought to thought

The novel is divided into four sections presented from four different points of view—three Compson family brothers and the

Compson family servant, Dilsey. The Compson family represents the Old South and all of its values—honor, virtue, and an understanding that blacks and whites are not equal. In the novel, Caddy Compson becomes pregnant out of wedlock, bringing shame and disgrace to her family. Through the perspectives of each of her brothers, we see how the values of the Old South are challenged and ultimately superseded by the tides of social change, from the forces of the Civil War to the new pragmatism of the industrial era and beyond. It is only through the perspective of her brother Benjy, a thirty-three-year-old mentally disabled man, that we catch a fragmented yet compassionate glimpse of Caddy's courage and beauty.

Stream of Consciousness Pioneers

Faulkner wasn't the first writer to use stream of consciousness in his writing. The Irish writer James Joyce and the English writer Virginia Woolf were pioneers of this kind of writing. James Joyce's novel *Ulysses* (1922) and Woolf's *To the Lighthouse* (1927) are landmark works of the style. Faulkner's brand of stream of consciousness, though, is considered the easiest to read.

The entire action takes place over three days during Easter weekend in 1928, and a flashback to 1910. Here's a tidy map of the book to help you if you're feeling bold and want to tackle it:

CHRONOLOGY	NARRATOR	NOTABLE ACTION
Section 1: April 7, 1928 (Good Friday; the past)	Benjy Compson	Benjy, thirty-three years old and mentally disabled, shifts from memory to memory, triggered by smells, tastes, or words. He has no concept of time. Something triggers his memory to a time when his sister Caddy climbed a tree (the only one of her siblings brave enough) to catch a glimpse of their grandmother's wake; Quentin remembers looking up at her muddy underwear.
Section 2: June 2, 1910 (The day Quentin commits suicide; the past)	Quentin Compson	Quentin, a student at Harvard University, is about to commit suicide. He can't accept that Caddy has lost her virginity and become pregnant. He sees it as a loss of honor for his family.
Section 3: April 6, 1928 (Saturday before Easter; the past)	Jason Compson	Jason Compson, the most corrupt brother, steals money his sister Caddy is sending to her teenager daughter. Through his perspective the reader learns that Caddy is divorced, Quentin drowned himself, and Benjy was castrated.
Section 4: April 8, 1928 (Easter Sunday; the present)	Dilsey	Dilsey, the family's servant. Hers is the most coherent narration and perspective. Dilsey reflects how the Compson family is destroyed by its corruption, greed, and obsession over honor: "I seed de beginnin, en now I sees de endin," she says.

Yoknapatawpha County

Nearly all of Faulkner's works deal with the South. Many of them are set in a fictional place, Yoknapatawpha County, a place marked by deep poverty and a clan-based society. Families fight for their honor and take special pride in their ancestry. Faulkner's novel *Sartoris*, published the same year as *The Sound and the Fury*, is the first of nineteen novels Faulkner wrote that are based in Yoknapatawpha County, tracing the decline and eventual decay of Southern genteel society. This exhaustive fictional exploration of the South and its myths and reality, rise and decline, is why Faulkner is considered a "writer of the South."

Faulkner As Screenwriter

Faulkner's other notable works are *As I Lay Dying* (1930), *Absalom, Absalom!* (1936), and *Go Down, Moses* (1942). Faulkner wrote works in almost every major genre. For a brief period, he even wrote screenplays in Hollywood—mostly to make money. Among the most acclaimed of these was *The Big Sleep*, starring Humphrey Bogart, based on a novel by Raymond Chandler.

Faulkner and the Modernist Worldview

Faulkner took the phrase "sound and fury" from Shakespeare's play *Macbeth* (Act 5, Scene 5):

Life's but a walking shadow, a poor player
That struts and frets his hour upon the stage,
And then is heard no more: it is a tale
Told by an idiot, full of sound and fury,
Signifying nothing.

Macbeth speaks these words in the last act after he learns his wife Lady Macbeth has died, and when he is finally reduced to a hollow man consumed by anxiety, fear, and paranoia. These lines express a pessimistic view of nature—sort of like the naturalists in the nineteenth century (from the previous chapter).

Whether life has any certain meaning or not, and if it does, what that meaning is—these were key questions that modernists asked themselves and explored in their works.

Faulkner might say life did have meaning—that there were universal truths that existed in the heart of all individuals, and writers could express them if they wrote works generated by the heart. His worldview could be much more optimistic than Macbeth's.

Faulkner was forty-nine years old before he won widespread acclaim for his writing. Up until that point, people considered him a token eccentric and too far from the mainstream to be of any real significance. Eventually, he won three major literary prizes: the Nobel Prize in Literature in 1950, the National Book Award in 1951 and 1955, and the Pulitzer Prize for Fiction in 1955.

WILLA CATHER AND JOHN STEINBECK

Writers of the West

"There was nothing but land: not a country at all, but the material out of which countries are made."

—Willa Cather, *My Ántonia*

The rich tradition of American realism and regionalism begun in the nineteenth century by writers such as Mark Twain continued well into the twentieth century with a new focus: life on the American prairie. With the country pretty much settled, and westward expansion complete, a new social fabric had begun developing in these fresh parts of the country.

Writers captured the rich beauty of the prairie landscapes, and the fears and anxieties of the settlers, migrant workers, and hobos who roamed it, and the social and economic forces that trapped them. Two writers, Willa Cather and John Steinbeck, captured some of these new realities best.

WILLA CATHER

Willa Cather (1873–1947) became one of the most famous writers of Midwestern regionalism in the early twentieth century. Her popular prairie trilogy gave readers a glimpse into the Nebraska landscape of the late nineteenth century and the courage and spirit of the prairie people scratching out their lives there.

Interestingly, Cather only spent a fraction of her life living on the prairie. She moved to Nebraska from Virginia when she was nine years old but she left as a young woman. She wrote her famous prairie novels in New York City, where she lived after the age of thirty-three. By the time Cather was writing her novels, the landscape and society of the prairie she knew as a child and young adult had drastically changed.

My Ántonia

Though it wasn't the most popular of her novels, *My Ántonia* (1918) survives as one of Cather's finest. The novel tells two stories typical of the era: that of the foreign immigrant and that of the American migrant. Cather traces their experiences, which are both similar and tragically different.

Ántonia Shimerda is a Bohemian immigrant whose family has moved to America searching for a better life. Jim Burden is an orphan from Virginia who is forced to move there after his parents die. Both are brought to the Nebraska prairie as children. Through their lives, readers see the loneliness and isolation these pioneers endured, the courage and independence they earned from their experiences, and the community that they relied on to survive.

Ántonia's and Jim's lives become entwined when Ántonia's father commits suicide under the pressures of prairie life. Her father was never convinced that coming to America was a great idea—his wife drove the family there with the hope that they would become rich. Jim's family owns a house, the emblem of stability, while Ántonia's father was never able to build one. Cather's novel, like other modernist stories, underscores the emptiness of the American dream. Her father dies longing for his true home, unable to find meaning in the New World.

> "The wagon jolted on, carrying me I knew not whither. I don't think I was homesick. If we never arrived anywhere, it did not matter. Between that earth and sky I felt erased, blotted out. I did not say my prayers that night: here, I felt, what would be would be."

—Willa Cather, *My Ántonia*

Ántonia, however, survives. Her endurance, courage, and persistence become the true symbol of the value of prairie life.

JOHN STEINBECK

While Cather's novels told of the prairie life in the late nineteenth century, the stories of John Steinbeck (1902–1968) told of life on the prairie in the early twentieth century—and what happened when catastrophe struck in the 1930s.

Dirty Thirties

In the 1930s, disaster struck the Midwestern prairies. In what became known as the Dirty Thirties or the Dust Bowl, severe droughts hit, dust storms swept through the area, and millions of farmers were displaced. Over 100 million acres across the Great Plains were affected. Families abandoned their farms, loaded up their belongings, and headed west to look for work. The country was scattered with migrants carrying all of their belongings through thick clouds of dust.

The calamity occurred because after five decades farmers still hadn't figured out the ecology of the prairie and developed farming practices suitable to the area. They didn't know that prairie grass was a vital part of the topsoil and that the vast web of roots of the prairie grass trapped moisture in the soil and kept the soil in place. For years farmers recklessly churned up the land with mechanized farming equipment, disrupting the topsoil to the point that it collapsed into dust.

The clouds of dust were so thick and black that people called them "black blizzards." Dust traveled far and wide, some of it even reaching the front lawn of the White House. The term *dust bowl* even entered the dictionary, meaning any region that is affected by drought and dust storms.

The Ecology of the Dust Bowl

In 1935, the botanist Paul Sears published a book called *Deserts on the March* to try to explain the ecology behind the tragedy and warn people from repeating their mistakes.

Steinbeck and the Okies

Moved by their plight, Steinbeck decided to write about the migrants' journey west. To research the book, Steinbeck drove to Oklahoma and joined the migrant workers on their trek to California to find work. What he saw affected him deeply. He watched Okies (the term for migrants from Oklahoma) linger in starvation as resentful Californians refused to give them food. Steinbeck condemned the Californians' actions as a "crime that goes beyond denunciation."

The Grapes of Wrath

Steinbeck shaped their experiences into his masterpiece novel, *The Grapes of Wrath*. When it was published in 1939, it catapulted Steinbeck to fame and secured his literary status as one of the most important writers of the twentieth century. The public was captivated by Steinbeck's story of the fictional Joads, a tenant-farm family from Oklahoma displaced during the Dust Bowl. Their heartbreaking story represented the stories of many Okies who lost their homes and went to California searching for work, only to find that the Great Depression had obliterated any chance of finding work there, too.

Written in Pencil

Steinbeck used 300 pencils to write his novel *East of Eden*. Typewriters existed then, but Steinbeck preferred to write by pencil.

The story blends naturalism and symbolism to tell of the exploitation of the displaced farmers. As a novel of naturalism, it depicts how the farmers' fate was ultimately shaped by the forces of the agricultural system in America at the time. The novel ends on one of the most shocking images in American literature: a woman breastfeeding a starving man. Her act is a symbol of selfless charity and compassion that stands in counterpoint to the ruthless exploitation practiced by businessmen throughout the book.

Over half a million copies of the book were sold—and that was just in the United States. Steinbeck won a Pulitzer Prize and National Book Award among other top prizes for the work.

A Compassionate Writer

Steinbeck felt that the job of a writer, above all, was to "communicate." He believed that, at its core, "writing may simply be a method or technique for communicating with other individuals," and in his Nobel Banquet speech he says the aim of writer should be "exposing [humanity's] many grievous faults and failures, with dredging up to the light our dark and dangerous dreams for the purpose of improvement." At the core of Steinbeck's writing is always a strong streak of compassion and a plea for people to become aware of the forces that blind them from ultimately understanding each other, the way to our truest salvation.

Of Mice and Men

Steinbeck's novel *Of Mice and Men* is another story about migrant workers, published two years before *The Grapes of Wrath*, in 1937. Steinbeck based the novel on his own experiences as a "bindlestiff" (migrant worker) as a young man. The first draft of the novel was eaten by his dog, Max.

Like Hemingway, Steinbeck used a simple style. As a result, his novels are relatively easy to read and became popular with the public. Although it took a long time for the literary establishment to welcome him (they felt his popularity meant he wasn't a "literary" author), he eventually was awarded the Nobel Prize in Literature in 1962.

Dust Bowl Fiction

The Grapes of Wrath is one of the most famous examples of Dust Bowl fiction, the term used to describe the novels and short stories that captured the catastrophe of the Dirty Thirties. Another example is *The Golden Bowl* (1937) by Frederick Manfred, whose protagonist goes back to the Dust Bowl to "try again." In 1941, writer James Agee collaborated with photographer Walker Evans to create *Let Us Now Praise Famous Men*, a chronicle of the lives of poor sharecroppers caught up in the Depression. Along with the work of photographers, playwrights, and other artists, their work created a cultural iconography of the era.

ROBERT FROST

America's Regional Poets

Robert Frost (1874–1963) is one of America's most beloved poets. Who doesn't recognize the lines, "Two roads diverged in a yellow wood" or "Miles to go before I sleep"? Perhaps you've even used them yourself in conversation. Frost's poems have become so popular that they have become ingrained in our American idiom. So much a part of America did Frost's poems become that, in 1960, John F. Kennedy invited him to read his poem "The Gift Outright" at Kennedy's presidential inauguration.

Robert Frost wrote during the time of Pound and Eliot and was a friend of Pound's. (Remember, Pound threw Frost over his shoulder in a jujitsu maneuver.) Pound admired Frost's poetry, even though their styles and subject matter were very different.

While Pound and Eliot were writing their modernist poetry, filled with obscure allusion and difficulty, Frost was working toward something different. Frost didn't like the abstraction and overt high-mindedness he saw in Eliot's and Pound's poetry; he wanted to bring poetry back to Earth—literally and figuratively.

Frost's Style

Frost felt that the poet, by using traditional forms, could restore sense and order to a world in chaos. Generally, Frost's poetry is characterized by:

- Clear diction
- Traditional forms such as the sonnet and the rhyming couplet
- Blank verse

- Colloquialism
- Natural rhythms
- Regionalism

Blank verse is made up of iambic pentameters (five iambic feet per line). Many major writers—Shakespeare, Milton, and Wordsworth—used blank verse, a highly adaptable meter. Frost used blank verse because it allowed him to capture the natural rhythms of colloquial speech.

Frost also believed that poetry should strive to match "sound to sense." By this Frost meant that poetry, in its use of meter, rhythm, rhyme, and sound, should reveal the meanings of the poem. Frost's masterful tuning of sound to sense has a lot to do with why his poetry is so popular.

Language of the New Englander

Frost created a folksy, natural poetry grounded in the New England landscape. But for all of its cheery bucolic descriptions of New England pastures, flowers, and farm life, there is a strain of melancholy and a probing of the dark underbelly of life. For Frost was still a child of modernism after all, writing after World War I, and he had to answer to society's alienated mood.

Life Is Lovely, Dark, and Deep

In his poetry, Frost uses nature to explore the universe. Some people have compared Frost with the American transcendentalists, since much of his work focuses on nature. But while the transcendentalists saw nature as an expression of God, Frost saw that nature had "no expression, nothing to express." Thematically, Frost more resembles Hawthorne and Melville in the way they use nature to search out the darker aspects of nature and the human heart, and Stephen Crane in the way he sees nature as ultimately indifferent and irrational.

Stopping by Woods

In his poem "Stopping by Woods on a Snowy Evening" (1923), Frost describes a woodland scene in winter. The speaker is being led through the snow in a horse-drawn carriage when he stops the horse to watch the snowfall. "My little horse must think it's queer / To stop without a farmhouse near," the speaker muses. The poem ends with the poet in reflection:

> The woods are lovely, dark and deep
> But I have promises to keep,
> And miles to go before I sleep.
> And miles to go before I sleep.

The sounds in the poem, and the repetition of the last two lines, clue the reader that this is more than just an ordinary scene in the woods and underscores a somber tone.

What does the poem mean? In Frost's poems, it's never quite easy to tell. Frost's language is sparklingly simple, but it always leaves a feeling that there's something dark and shapeless looming underneath it. Some people read the poem as a meditation on death. Frost agreed, but said that wasn't exactly what he intended (that's for you to decide).

Other popular poems of Frost's include "The Road Not Taken," "Mending Wall," and "Fire and Ice." Some of his poems, such as "The Death of the Hired Man," are longer and more story based.

Frost suffered a lot of tragedy in his life: Two of his children died young, another committed suicide, a daughter died after childbirth, and another daughter suffered a nervous breakdown. At one point Frost became suicidal himself.

He lived a long life—he died when he was eighty-nine. Over his life, he was widely celebrated for his poetry and won four Pulitzer Prizes.

EDWIN ARLINGTON ROBINSON

Edwin Arlington Robinson (1869–1935) is another New England poet, like Frost, who explores darker themes in his work. Like Frost, he used traditional forms to craft his poetry, and featured ordinary people from New England in his poems.

In his famous poem "Richard Cory" (1897), Robinson created the character of the person who "has it all" but feels nothing inside. The poem ends with the title character's suicide:

> And so we worked, and waited for the light,
> And went without the meat, and cursed the bread;
> And Richard Cory, one calm summer night,
> Went home and put a bullet through his head.

Robinson's depiction of Richard Cory presented a jarring image of quiet, sophisticated New England. Underneath its pretty, snowy winter landscapes rang a message like a bullet through the head: The modern world can be one of utter despair.

CARL SANDBURG AND THE CHICAGO POETS

Up until the turn of the century, New England was considered the center of the literary establishment. Carl Sandburg and the Chicago poets challenged that notion by creating vibrant poetic works that represented the Midwest. They created verse that celebrated

Chicago, which had become a thriving city and a cultural hub in its own right.

The three major poets of the Chicago school, Carl Sandburg (1878–1967), Edgar Lee Masters (1868–1950), and Vachel Lindsay (1879–1931), all used relaxed colloquial language and realism. Their poetry explored the dialects, inner lives, and populist sentiments that defined Midwestern culture in the early twentieth century.

Spoon River

Edgar Lee Masters's *Spoon River Anthology* (1915) features 250 Midwestern people who all share one thing: They are dead. Safe in death, these people are now free to speak honestly about the despair, failures, and lost dreams they experienced during life.

The regional poets of the first half of the twentieth century put their own mark on modernism by re-exploring America through its landscape and the inner lives of its "regular" people. Just like Whitman, these poets gave voice to the people, but the voices were now more fragmented and tinged with despair as the hopes and dreams of America were chastened by the horrors of major world wars.

E.E. CUMMINGS AND
WILLIAM CARLOS WILLIAMS

Experimental Poets

Some of the most innovative poetry in America came out of the modernist era. Poets such as T.S. Eliot and Ezra Pound sounded the call, and a steady stream of poets replied. By the 1920s, American poetry was well on its way to a new voice, tenor, and style that captured and defined the new era.

E.E. Cummings

The most obvious poetic innovator was the poet E.E. Cummings (1894–1962). He played with typography—the way type appears on a page—as well as grammar, spelling, punctuation, rhythm, and form (pretty much all the rules of language), often spelling his own name in all-lowercase letters. His highly idiosyncratic style was a visual symbol of nonconformity and underscored the experimental tone of the era.

"It takes courage to grow up and become who you really are."

—e.e. cummings

It can be easy to forget that poetry is not just an act of silently reading words on a page. A poem is a written work *meant to be spoken.* (Next time you read a poem, try reading it silently and then aloud and note the difference!) The *way* the lines break, *where* they break across the page—these are all part of the way the poem is *meant to be read by the eyes*.

The eyes and ear are both involved in the meaning-making magic that is reading poetry.

What a poem *says* is a product of *how* it says it.

Think of how Emily Dickinson's poetry is altered when periods replace her characteristic dashes—when editors replace the dashes with periods, the hesitancy and expectation in her poetry was blunted. And think of Frost's careful balancing of *sound* to *sense*— these are all conscious acts creating the experience of poetry.

Cummings made this more obvious in his poetry. He played with nearly all of the things that go into making a poem. Here's an example:

> i carry your heart with me(i carry it in
> my heart)i am never without it(anywhere
> i go you go,my dear;and whatever is done
> by only me is your doing,my darling)
>   i fear

No, those aren't mistakes—the "i" is meant to be lowercase; those missing spaces between the words in every line are intentional. So what does it mean?

That's the beauty of E.E. Cummings—his poetry is so playful that once you begin to think about it the possibilities seem endless! The lowercase "i" could signal the diminution of the self, the lack of missing spaces underscoring the closeness with which the speaker carries his love's heart to his own (right up against the chest even!). And all that white space in the last line of the stanza—the speaker's fear made visible.

In all, E.E. Cummings published more than 2,000 poems. With shrewd planning, he was able to stretch his money enough to devote his life to his poetry and live as a bohemian artist in the Roaring Twenties. He used money he earned from literary prizes (which were many) and money loaned to him by his parents to keep himself afloat. He was never interested in celebrity or wealth.

Cummings is seen as a vibrant nonconformist and dynamic part of the romantic tradition—a true heir to the innovativeness of Whitman. Interestingly, though, underneath all that nonconformity, Cummings was kind of a conservative. Late in his life, after a trip to the Soviet Union in 1931, he became disillusioned with socialist politics and turned towards Republicanism.

William Carlos Williams

Poet William Carlos Williams (1883–1963) also received Pound's dictate to "make it new" and did just that. Much of the innovation that Pound called for and put into motion with his imagism movement found its expression in Williams's highly innovative poetry. In a sense, Williams became "more Pound than Pound," since as innovative as Pound was, Williams felt he hadn't gone far enough. Pound's influence was so strong during the early twentieth century, Williams said he could divide his life into "Before Pound" and "After Pound."

Dr. Williams

Unlike E.E. Cummings, William Carlos Williams's principle job wasn't as a poet. He was a trained physician. He became chief of pediatrics at a hospital in New Jersey in his forties, a position in which he served until his death.

Like Eliot and Pound, Williams wanted to see poetry stripped of all traces of the "establishment" and given a sense of the "disestablishment" that characterized the modernist era. He wanted poetry to have a basis in the language as it was spoken. He said, "we are *through* with the iambic pentameter . . . through with the measured quatrain" and through "with the sonnet" (at least as it was used at the time). Big words for a poet.

Above all, he wanted poetry to communicate *directly*. As a result, his poetry became highly imagistic. Here are some lines from one of his most popular poems, "The Red Wheelbarrow":

so much depends
upon

a red wheel
barrow

glazed with rain

The entire poem rests on one image: the red wheelbarrow.

Enjambment

When a poet breaks a line at a place other than at its grammatical end it is called enjambment. *Enjambment* comes from the French word *enjambment*, which means "to stride across" (*jambe* = leg). Lines that don't use enjambment are called "end-stopped." Enjambment can create all sorts of tension in the poem since where the words stop at the end of the line doesn't match up with the grammatical stopping point.

"The Red Wheelbarrow" does many innovative things. Like Cummings, Williams uses lowercase letters. He uses unusually short lines. The line breaks (enjambment) slow the reader down, which mirrors what the poem is doing itself—slowing down to consider how much "depends upon a red wheelbarrow." The poem strips away literary pretense, which forces the reader to look carefully at the words, and also anew at the things that surround him or her. Williams creates a highly meditative poem anchored by a concrete central image.

E.E. Cummings and William Carlos Williams are just two of the modernist era's innovative poets. There are many others.

The poet Wallace Stevens also wrote highly meditative and imagistic poetry that focused on ideas and consciousness. His work is philosophical and his language is spare and precise. He won a Pulitzer Prize for his work in 1955.

Hart Crane, who died at the young age of thirty-two, set out with a massive ambition to write the "American poem." His long poem "The Bridge," which takes the Brooklyn Bridge as its central image, is an epic poem that captures the mood of the era like T.S. Eliot's "The Waste Land," but in a more optimistic mood.

In all, the innovative poets of modernism created dynamic works that captured the sense of fluctuation, confusion, and dynamic energy of the era itself.

THE HARLEM RENAISSANCE

The Flowering of African-American Literature

"There is no lack within the Negro people of beauty, strength, and power."

—Langston Hughes

From 1915 to 1929, a burst of African-American writing and creativity flowered in the North. A diverse group of black writers created novels, autobiographies, poetry, and political literature that shaped the modern era of black American writing. The period is now referred to as the Harlem Renaissance.

MIGRATION NORTH

After World War I, thousands of African Americans began moving from the farms of the South to the cities of the North. During the brief period of economic prosperity in the 1920s, cities such as Chicago and New York City were full of job openings and opportunities attracting African Americans from the South with the hope of a better life.

Harlem Becomes a Lightning Rod

This migration sparked a period of highly innovative ideas, music, and spirited calls for social change in major cities across the

North. The neighborhood of Harlem in New York City's Manhattan became a rich cultural hub where African-American intellectuals, writers, and artists fed off each other's ideas and creative work. The nonconformist attitudes, new fashions, and unconventional life-styles that typified this "anything goes" era of the 1920s took shape in Harlem in an explosion of new African-American literature.

Rebirth

The word *renaissance* comes from a French word meaning "rebirth." Literary and cultural movements that represent cultural "rebirths" are usually given the term "renaissance." The Harlem Renaissance was given its name because it was seen as a rebirth of African-American arts and culture in America.

RICHARD WRIGHT

Richard Wright (1908–1960) became one of the most distinguished African-American authors of the Harlem Renaissance. His masterpiece novel *Native Son* immediately sold a quarter of a million copies when it was published in 1940. The controversial novel posed a very difficult question to readers: When is violence a personal necessity?

Bigger's Plight

Native Son follows a twenty-one-year-old African-American man named Bigger who takes a job as a chauffeur with the wealthy white Dalton family. Bigger lives in a Chicago tenement and typified many young black American males that filled northern cities looking to prosper.

Things fall apart when Bigger accidentally kills Mary Dalton, the family's beautiful daughter. After driving Mary home one night, Bigger has to carry her inside because she is too drunk to walk. Roused awake, Mrs. Dalton, who is blind, comes into Mary's room as Bigger is putting her to bed. Realizing he'll likely be accused of rape for being in her room, he accidentally suffocates Mary in a frantic attempt to quiet her with a pillow. Bigger is now caught, metaphorically: He falls into a cycle of violence spurred by fear and racial conflict.

The Jazz Age

Running alongside the Harlem Renaissance was the Jazz Age. A highly innovative time for music, the Jazz Age saw the rise of jazz, a style of music characterized by syncopated rhythms, improvisation, and a highly lively tone. Jazz developed and flourished in clubs across Chicago and New York during the 1920s. Musicians like Duke Ellington and Louis Armstrong became famous figures of the Jazz Age.

In the end, Bigger is able to come to a greater understanding of the people and forces that drove him to his fate. Even though he is sentenced to death, he dies with dignity and courage.

Wright's book exploded people's complacency about black issues in America. Wright painted a vivid and uncomfortable picture of issues such as inequality, racism, and violence—reading his novel can be a tough experience.

Eventually, like many other writers of the modernist movement, Wright became disillusioned with America and escaped to Paris. The City of Light proved to be a good home for Wright: The French lauded him as a great writer, ranking him with Hemingway, Faulkner, and Fitzgerald.

Return to Naturalism

Native Son is like other books of naturalism—a character is locked in complex societal forces that ultimately determine his fate.

ZORA NEALE HURSTON

Another famous writer to come out of the Harlem Renaissance was Zora Neale Hurston (1891–1960). Hurston became a voice of African-American women. Much of her work uses African-American folklore to explore themes relating to black identity in the early twentieth century.

Preserving African-American Folklore

Hurston became interested in African-American folklore while she was a student at Barnard College. After graduating in 1927, she won a fellowship to study at Columbia University in order to continue her studies of black oral traditions. Hurston used her anthropological studies to create *Mules and Men* (1935), an autoethnographical (recall the term *autoethnography* from Chapter 1!) account of African-American folklore, and her masterpiece, *Their Eyes Were Watching God* (1937).

Their Eyes Were Watching God

Their Eyes Were Watching God is about a young black Southern woman's journey to find and claim her identity. Hurston based Janie's experiences on the stories she heard and also her own experience with a strong but abusive lover. Janie is of mixed race and finds tensions both within the white and black communities.

Not Political Enough

When it was published, some black writers criticized Hurston for not being bold enough in her characterization. Richard Wright said her characters operated in a "narrow and safe orbit in which America likes to see the Negro live." Authors such as Wright were using their writing to bring much-needed light to critical sociopolitical issues facing African Americans. They considered anything other than that a waste, or worse, a failure.

One of the Top 100

Their Eyes Were Watching God made it in *Time* magazine's All-Time 100 Novels, which was a list of the 100 best novels published from 1923 to 2005. Oprah Winfrey produced a film version of the novel starring the actress Halle Berry in 2005.

It wasn't until years later, when scholars began to focus on the importance of the resurgence of African-American folk traditions during the Harlem Renaissance, that Hurston's work was seen in a new light.

LANGSTON HUGHES

Perhaps the most popular literary figure to come out of the Harlem Renaissance was Langston Hughes (1902–1967). Hughes was a successful poet and author of the twenties and is still popular today.

Hughes's bright, smiling face is one of the most recognizable faces in literature, and has become an iconic image of the lively energy of the Jazz Age.

Jazz Poet

Like Hurston, Hughes wanted to capture the oral traditions and folklore of African Americans. In his poetry, Hughes tried to capture the rhythms of jazz:

Droning a drowsy syncopated tune,
Rocking back and forth to a mellow croon,
    I heard a Negro play.
Down on Lenox Avenue the other night
By the pale dull pallor of an old gas light
    He did a lazy sway ...
    He did a lazy sway ...
—"The Weary Blues"

Hughes's writing aimed to unite black people by inspiring pride in their traditions.

Political Voices

Booker T. Washington and W.E.B. Du Bois are two important political voices of the nineteenth and twentieth centuries; the positions they outlined in the debate over African-American progress continue today. Washington wanted blacks to focus on bettering themselves through education and hard work, putting discrimination aside. Du Bois disagreed—he felt that ignoring discrimination would only perpetuate it. Du Bois became a founder of the NAACP—a key civil rights organization for African Americans.

GREAT DEPRESSION ENDS THE PARTY FOR EVERYONE

Of course, all great things must come to an end, and with the stock market crash of 1929, the Harlem Renaissance came to a close. Though things changed, the works of the Harlem Renaissance still survive as living voices of the African-American experience at the start of the twentieth century.

Chapter 7

Postwar Literature

After the Great Depression of the thirties and the end of World War II in 1945, America entered a period of relative calmness, stability, and conformity. American literature and culture responded by being anything but.

In the 1940s and 1950s, a small group of writers, disparagingly termed "beatniks," started writing works that were obscene and experimental, and openly discussed almost every taboo topic under the sun. Underneath all of the raucousness of their writings lay an important message: Despair still runs through American culture. Their writings reflected how, in exchange for stability and comfort, Americans had traded their source of vitality—creativity.

In the late 1950s and early 1960s, poetry began to explore this message from another angle: the personal "I." A new type of poetry called confessional poetry developed that discussed subject matters considered taboo for the politically conservative era—topics such as depression, death, and relationships—from a deeply personal and intimate perspective. The works of Anne Sexton, Sylvia Plath, and Robert Lowell ushered in a new style that influenced writers for decades to come.

And let's not forget the dramatists of the twentieth century—they came into their own during this period as well. Eugene O'Neill, Tennessee Williams, and Arthur Miller became three of the most important dramatists of the period. Their works explored the idea of family in America and often asked questions such as: How does the American dream affect the family unit? In what ways do the pressures of society play out in the family dynamic? These dramatists show how American society in the twentieth century could fracture the line between reality and fantasy and rupture the bonds between family members.

Finally, the gothic made a resurgence in the twentieth century—this time turning its attention toward the South. The gothic tradition in America begun by writers like Edgar Allan Poe began to emerge in the writings of William Faulkner, Flannery O'Connor, and other writers who explored the South. Their works show how the decay of Southern genteel society and the rise of modern society created tension. Writers were now less focused on the evils of Southern society and more on the quiet yet sinister aspects that stemmed from the sense of alienation and loss in the modern world. Flannery O'Connor's use of the grotesque and humor made her one of the more unique Southern voices in modern literature.

THE BEATS AND J.D. SALINGER

The Counterculture Club

While the Lost Generation was "lost," the Beat Generation was just
... beat. These were the people who grew up during the Depression,
survived World War II, and came of age during a time of calm but
stifling conformity. The beats experimented with drugs, sexuality,
Eastern philosophies—all in an attempt to find what they saw was
desperately missing in culture: a sense of vitality and creativity.

"Dean and I were embarked on a journey through post-Whitman America to
FIND that America and to FIND the inherent goodness in American man. . . . It
was really a story about 2 Catholic buddies roaming the country in search of
God. And we found him."

—Jack Kerouac, *Letters: 1957–1969*

The Beat Movement Is Born

As with many literary movements, the beat movement started
with a small group of friends sitting around apartments and bars
talking about life, art, and literature. Jack Kerouac, Allen Ginsberg,
and William S. Burroughs were three writers who met in the New
York City underground in 1944. They were all, in their different ways,
father figures of the beat movement and spokesmen for the homeless, the hip, and the spirit of a new Beat Generation in the 1950s.

The Word *Beat*

The term *beat* had many meanings to the Beat Generation: Kerouac said he first heard the term used by his friend Herbert Huncke who said he was "beat" by his street-hustling lifestyle. The term was also a reference to the jazz "beat" and the "beatific" (ecstatic/holy) aims of the movement. The beats were formally christened when journalist John Clellon Holmes (a friend of Kerouac's) published his famous article "This Is the Beat Generation" in the *New York Times*.

JACK KEROUAC

Jack Kerouac (1922–1969) was born in Lowell, a depressed mill town in Massachusetts. On the outside, Kerouac was the most "all-American" of the beats. He was handsome, athletic, and social.

In an effort to keep his family from abject poverty, Kerouac tried to win a football scholarship to college. He ended up getting one to Columbia University, so the family packed up and moved together to New York. When it was clear he wasn't going to get any game time, Kerouac dropped out and joined the merchant marines. During his time off, he routinely came back to New York to visit the friends he made during his time at Columbia—Ginsberg, Burroughs, and an ex-convict named Neal Cassady.

On the Road

Kerouac was determined to become a writer. After seven years of work and revision, in 1957 he finally published his novel, *On the Road*, the bible of the Beat Generation and a major work of the beat movement. Kerouac based the novel on several road trips he took with Neal Cassady, who became another seminal figure of the beats after Kerouac immortalized him in the novel.

The novel was written in a stream-of-consciousness style to capture the spontaneity of living "on the road." In Kerouac's novel, the true place of freedom is on the road, without empty commitments. The only commitment is to the journey.

In order to avoid interrupting his flow of work, Kerouac taped pages together and fed them through his typewriter instead of inserting pages sheet by sheet. Kerouac shrewdly cultivated an image of himself writing in a feverish fit of divine inspiration by claiming in interviews he wrote the book in three weeks on this one continuous scroll of paper.

On the Road had a huge effect on culture in the fifties and sixties, and beyond. It survives as a cult favorite. Many famous musicians and authors such as Bob Dylan, Jim Morrison, and Hunter S. Thompson have claimed it as an influence on their work.

"Better to sleep in an uncomfortable bed free, than sleep in a comfortable bed unfree."

—Jack Kerouac, *On the Road*

WILLIAM S. BURROUGHS

Kerouac and Ginsberg considered their friend, William S. Burroughs (1914–1997), their literary father. Burroughs was certainly the most extreme of the bunch—both in his writing and in his life.

Burroughs came from a wealthy family—his grandfather invented an adding machine (an early calculator) and established a successful business corporation in the 1800s. In 1936, after Burroughs graduated from Harvard University with an English degree, his parents set him up with a fat allowance, which allowed him to live work-free for years. He spent his time doing drugs, mingling with prostitutes and drug dealers, and inspiring artists around him.

Burroughs became a frequenter of the New York underworld in the 1940s, where he met Kerouac and Ginsberg. Life caught up to Burroughs in 1949 when he was arrested on drug charges. He decided to escape to Mexico with his wife, Joan; they grew pot together, and Burroughs began a postgraduate degree in anthropology.

The Severed Finger

Burroughs cut off his left pinky finger when he was twenty-five, claiming it was part of an initiatory rite of the Crow Indian tribe. A psychiatrist admitted Burroughs to a mental hospital after Burroughs showed him his severed finger.

Burroughs found himself in trouble again after he shot and killed his wife during a botched re-enactment of the William Tell legend. He was able to avoid jail time when the judge ruled that the death was an accident, but he spent the rest of the fifties and sixties wandering Europe and North Africa. Burroughs later reflected that he "would have never become a writer but for Joan's death. . . . So the death of Joan brought me into contact with the invader, the Ugly Spirit, and maneuvered me into a lifelong struggle, in which I have had no choice except to write my way out."

Naked Lunch
In 1959, Burroughs published his major work, *Naked Lunch*. The book is based on his experiences and is narrated by his alter

ego, William Lee. The extremely controversial book had its author charged with obscenity in Boston for its portrayals of pornography, rape, and drug use. In its tone, subject matter, and paranoia-like structure, the book became another seminal work of the Beat Generation.

ALLEN GINSBERG

Allen Ginsberg (1926 –1997) was the leading poet of the beats. His poetry collection *Howl* became the poetic center of the beat movement and gave voice to the spiritual yearnings and frustrations of the Beat Generation. Ginsberg was the most scholarly and quiet of the bunch, though no less provocative (at least compared to Kerouac—Burroughs takes the cake in that regard).

Like Kerouac, Ginsberg attended Columbia. When he began spending time with junkies and criminals, he found himself in trouble at the university. He was finally expelled when it was discovered he was drawing obscene pictures in the dust of his dormitory window to alert the cleaners it was time to come in.

After Burroughs was arrested for killing Joan, Ginsberg was scared straight for a time. He took a quiet job as a researcher and tried to become "normal." Of course, that didn't last long. Ginsberg finally left and headed to San Francisco where he immersed himself in the poetry scene and made it famous.

Howling at the Moon

"Hold back the edges of your gowns, Ladies, we are going through Hell." This was how the poet William Carlos Williams introduced Ginsberg's poetry collection *Howl* when it was published in 1956.

When Ginsberg read his *Howl* poems aloud at a reading in San Francisco in 1955, he instantly became a symbol of sexual deviancy. The poem's frank description of human sexuality and homosexuality outright disgusted the public. Here's its famous beginning:

I saw the best minds of my generation destroyed by madness,
   starving hysterical naked,
dragging themselves through the negro streets at dawn
   looking for an angry fix,

The public's reception of *Howl* mirrored Whitman's *Leaves of Grass* in many ways—like Whitman, Ginsberg was considered just another obscene poet. Both works are now, of course, considered classics.

Of all his peers, Ginsberg believed most in the experimentalism of the beats. He believed in the spiritual value of their exploration into the underworld and was convinced it was leading to a true poetic revelation.

J.D. SALINGER

Rounding out our literary voices of the young generation of the 1950s is Holden Caulfield, the fictional protagonist of *The Catcher in the Rye* (1951) by J.D. Salinger (1919–2010). Salinger's portrayal of teen angst is so convincing and sincere that many young people felt Salinger "knew" them and that they "knew" him—something that proved to be very annoying to the author. The enormous success of *The Catcher in the Rye* was so annoying, in fact, it sent Salinger fleeing to Cornish, a remote hill town in New Hampshire.

Salinger became one of America's most famous literary recluses. For years he refused to grant interviews or publish anything after his last collection of stories in 1961 (though he said he was still writing). When he died in 2010, everyone wanted to know who had access to his unpublished work and whether it would ever be published. Dozens of articles were published over these questions. The public is still hungry for a glimpse into this elusive hermit's life.

The Catcher in the Rye and Holden Caulfield still survive as the voice of disaffected youth. It's had more than forty printings, has sold millions of copies, and *still* sells over 200,000 copies a year.

CONFESSIONAL POETS

Poetry of the Personal

During the 1950s a style of poetry called confessional poetry began to take shape. The poets Robert Lowell, Sylvia Plath, and Anne Sexton became the face of this small but important movement. They discussed all of those things you discuss with your therapist.

Again, this movement started with a small group of people talking and working together in small spaces. This time it wasn't a bar; it was the classroom of Robert Lowell at Boston University in Massachusetts.

Robert Lowell was a creative-writing teacher at Boston University. Anne Sexton began taking his class after her therapist suggested she write poetry as a form of self-therapy. When Plath joined the class, they became friends. They both shared a history of mental illness, suicidal episodes, and a love of poetry.

Sexton began to develop a "confessional" style of poetry under the influence of Lowell and another poet named W.D. Snodgrass, who wrote a collection of deeply personal poetry called *Heart's Needle*. Sexton encouraged Sylvia, already a poet, to take her work in a similar direction. All three poets—Lowell, Plath, and Sexton—ended up feeding off each other's work and creating landmark works of the movement.

ROBERT LOWELL

Lowell (1917–1977) became the movement's leading figure when he published his book of poetry, *Life Studies*, in 1959. Though other poets (like Snodgrass) were beginning to write in this style, his work gained the most attention. Lowell was a famous and distinguished poet with enough influence to make the movement stick.

Life Studies discussed *really* personal topics like Lowell's relationships with his parents, his parents' marriage, and his emotional breakdowns. In one poem, "Waking in the Blue," Lowell describes his experience in McLean Hospital, a famous mental hospital in Massachusetts. For Lowell, who was from a prominent and distinguished New England family, writing poetry that discussed his nervous breakdown was a brave thing to do. Mental illness was something to hide, not openly discuss.

SYLVIA PLATH

"I've been very excited by what I feel is the new breakthrough that came with, say, Robert Lowell's *Life Studies*, this intense breakthrough into very serious, very personal, emotional experience which I feel has been partly taboo. Robert Lowell's poems about his experience in a mental hospital, for example, interested me very much." So says Sylvia Plath (1932–1963), one of Lowell's students, in an interview with Peter Orr in *The Poet Speaks: Interviews with Contemporary Poets*.

Plath is arguably the most famous figure of the confessional poets, which may have a lot to do with the grimly dramatic way she died: She locked herself in her kitchen, stuffed the doors, turned the gas on, and quietly put her head in the oven.

Plath's death sparked outrage in her readers and raised her to a cult figure of feminism. Lovers of Plath's poetry blamed Plath's husband, Ted Hughes, for her death, claiming he drove her to suicide. They cast Plath as a woman stifled by her husband and the demands of motherhood.

In fact, Plath had been suicidal before she met Hughes. After losing her father at age eight, she struggled throughout her short life with mental illness. Between her junior and senior years at Smith College, she tried to commit suicide by overdosing on sleeping pills.

After electroshock therapy, Plath returned to college, winning a Fulbright scholarship to study at Cambridge University in England (where she met Hughes). Plath was already a budding poet before she met Sexton and Lowell.

Sylvia's Death

During their friendship, Sexton and Plath confided in each other about their mental illness and suicide attempts. Sexton wrote a poem to commemorate Sylvia's suicide called "Sylvia's Death." She calls Sylvia a "Thief" for crawling "down alone / into the death I wanted so badly and for so long, / the death we said we both outgrew."

Daddy Dearest

Sylvia's poem "Daddy" is one of the most famous examples of confessional poetry, in part because of its shocking imagery, but also because of the masterful way Plath spins personal suffering into mythic, universal truths. (Freud could have a field day interpreting this poem.) Here's a glimpse:

There's a stake in your fat black heart
And the villagers never liked you.
They are dancing and stamping on you.
They always *knew* it was you.
Daddy, daddy, you bastard, I'm through.

In the poem, the speaker (ostensibly Plath herself) is caught in a brutal regime of her dead father's influence. She has "lived like a foot" in her father's "shoe," "Barely daring to breathe or Achoo." She searches for him as an outsider "In the German tongue, in the Polish town," and as herself, at age twenty: "At twenty I tried to die / And get back, back, back to you" (clearly a reference to her real-life suicide attempt at that age and an attempt to join him beyond the grave). After thirty years, the speaker is ready to free herself from her constructed image of her father: "I have always been scared of *you*, / With your Luftwaffe, your gobbledygoo. . . . daddy, I'm finally through."

Plath uses the imagery of Nazi Germany to illustrate the psychologically dominating influence her father's image casts over her, likening it to a Jew crushed by a Nazi. It is one powerful read.

ANNE SEXTON

Anne Sexton (1928–1974) also wrote provocative poetry of enormous depth and power. Sexton dug deep—she discussed her relationships with her husband and children, menstruation, abortion, masturbation, incest—all with characteristic emotional force and directness. Her poetry was raw and shocking, a key feature of confessional poetry.

Madness

Bedlam was the popular name for Bethlehem Royal Hospital, a hospital that served as a lunatic asylum in London beginning in the 1200s. The term now generally refers to "madness" or "chaos."

Sexton began writing poetry late—when she was in her late twenties. She had to ask a friend to come with her to her first poetry class. Within a short time she became enchanted by the sonnet and was writing poems daily. She published her first book of poems, *To Bedlam and Part Way Back*, in 1960 when she was forty years old.

Never quite at ease with the label "confessional," Sexton admitted that some of the material in her poetry was not actually true. For her, poetic technique and symbolic imagery trumped factual details.

Sexton was awarded well for her work. She won a Pulitzer Prize in 1966 for her collection *Live or Die*. After a while, though, her addiction to alcohol and sleeping pills began to interfere with her work. Some critics found her later poetry nothing more than "outspoken soap-opera." Sexton finally took her own life by locking herself in her garage with the car running in 1974. She was forty-six years old.

It's important to remember that confessional poetry was not simply a matter of airing one's dirty laundry or splitting a diary entry over a series of short lines and calling it a poem. Confessional poetry was a new poetic mode, the development of a new voice, through which a poet deeply probes personal subjects at a "poetic distance" from an "I" or "mask." These poets were and were not their speakers. In some cases their "confessions" weren't even true—which didn't matter so much as what was said was shaped into "poetic truths." These poets were—no question—highly skilled.

Today, confessional poetry survives in the works of writers such as Sharon Olds and Marie Howe, who talk frankly about female sexuality and AIDS.

TWENTIETH-CENTURY DRAMATISTS

Family and the American Dream

Much of the drama of the twentieth century centers around one theme: family. Here's a look at how three of the century's most accomplished dramatists explored this all-American theme.

EUGENE O'NEILL

Eugene O'Neill (1888–1953) was born in a hotel room and died in a hotel room. In fact, his last words were: "I knew it. I knew it. Born in a hotel room and died in a hotel room." A highly accomplished playwright, he raised drama to a respected literary medium in America.

The Haunting of Eugene O'Neill

The hotel O'Neill died in was the Sheraton Hotel, now a Boston University dormitory. Students claim that O'Neill's ghost still haunts the room where he died.

The son of a traveling stage actor, O'Neill was immersed in drama from a young age. Much of his youth was spent on the road with his father, who played a role in the touring production of *The Count of Monte Cristo*.

During his life, O'Neill enjoyed a long run as Broadway's leading playwright. His plays *Beyond the Horizon* (1920) and *Anna Christie*

(1922) both won Pulitzer Prizes. After the loss of his parents and brother he wrote *Desire Under the Elms* (1924) and *Strange Interludes* (1928). One of his greatest gifts was the ability to turn his personal anguish into dramatic power.

Long Day's Journey Into Night

It wasn't until 1956, three years after his death, however, that his greatest works saw the stage. In the 1940s, O'Neill began writing a semiautobiographical work, *Long Day's Journey Into Night*, about a family whose father was obsessed with having money and avoiding "dying in the poor house," and a mother whose dependence on morphine creates extreme anxiety in her sons. The work was so personal, O'Neill stipulated to his wife that the work was not to be published until twenty-five years after his death (obviously she didn't listen).

Oona and Charlie

In 1943, O'Neill's eighteen-year-old daughter Oona married Charlie Chaplin, who was fifty-four—the same age as her father. O'Neill was so angry he disinherited his daughter. (Fun fact: Chaplin stole her away from J.D. Salinger!) Oona and Charlie's daughter, Geraldine, became a distinguished actress, appearing in such movies as *Doctor Zhivago*, and Geraldine's daughter, named Oona after her grandmother, appeared in *Game of Thrones* (as Talisa, Robb Stark's wife, who was killed at the Red Wedding).

In 1936, O'Neill became the first dramatist to be awarded the Nobel Prize in Literature. The prize council honored O'Neill "for the power, honesty, and deep-felt emotion of his dramatic works, which embody an original concept of tragedy."

TENNESSEE WILLIAMS

The playwright Tennessee Williams (1911–1983) also grew up in a dysfunctional household like O'Neill and also had the power to turn his personal frustrations into dramatic masterpieces for the stage.

Thomas Williams was born in Mississippi in 1911. His father was a traveling shoe salesman with a wild temper, and his mother was a housewife with a dramatic personality and an obsession with "keeping up with the Joneses." As a result, his parents often fought.

After Tennessee's father got a promotion, the family moved to St. Louis, Missouri. The stress of the job and the move took a toll—his father began drinking heavily and became more abusive toward his wife and children. As a result, Tennessee spent his teen years in an increasingly turbulent household. Tennessee later reflected that the main source of tension in the household was his parents' marriage, which he described as "just a wrong marriage."

After a series of halfhearted attempts to work in business like his father, Williams moved to New Orleans at the age of twenty-eight. Determined to become a writer, he changed his name to Tennessee and began writing plays. In 1945, when he was thirty-four, Williams got his big break when his play *The Glass Menagerie* opened on Broadway.

The Glass Menagerie

The Glass Menagerie is about a Southern middle-aged woman living in a St. Louis tenement with her two children who are in their twenties. The woman was once a Southern debutante and is hyperfocused on the future of her daughter, who suffers a limp after a bout of polio and as a result is shy and withdrawn. The woman urges her son Tom to find someone for his sister, which he does—a coworker named Jim. When it doesn't work out, the mother cruelly lashes out at her son. The play ends with Tom leaving, wishing his sister well.

Williams based the play on the dynamics of his family life growing up, and based the woman on his mother. The play paints a picture of the decay of Southern genteel society and an obsession with social class and how they interfere with family bonds.

ARTHUR MILLER

Arthur Miller (1915–2005) is considered one of the greatest playwrights of the twentieth century. After witnessing the devastating effects the Depression had on his father, Miller became attuned to the deep sense of turmoil the Depression had on the American psyche. He created one of the most memorable figures in American drama: Willy Loman.

Willy Loman: America's Saddest Everyman

When Miller created his masterpiece, *Death of a Salesman*, he focused on making one thing clear: that his main character believed in the imagined reality of the past as much as the reality of the present. Willy Loman's stubborn belief in the American dream makes him a tragic hero and figure of empathy. In a way, Willy Loman is like Jay Gatsby; he symbolizes how the American dream can fracture the line between reality and illusion in the human mind.

Death of a Salesman

Loman is an aging Brooklyn salesman who can't come to terms with the fact that he is being thoughtlessly fired from a job he loyally served for thirty-four years and that his son, Biff, can't (and doesn't want to) find a job in sales. Even though he's just been dealt a humiliating blow by his company, Willy still sees business as the only way to success, while Biff sees it as a dead end: he'd rather work outside with his hands.

After a series of schizophrenic-like episodes in which Willy reminisces about the past (and escapes from his present situation), he begins to crack. In a moment of frustration, Biff tries to get Willy to come to terms with reality—that both he and his father are just average men who are destined for ordinary lives. "Pop," he says, "I'm nothing! I'm nothing, Pop. Can't you understand that? There's no spite in it any more. I'm just what I am, that's all." Willy resists, ultimately driven by shallowness and empty values. He is unable to establish a real relationship with his son because he is under the spell of another, more illusory reality—the American dream.

Mind and Body

In 1956, Miller married the actress and sex symbol Marilyn Monroe. Their marriage was troubled and ended in 1961, a year before Monroe's death. People called it a marriage of the "Great American Mind" to the "Great American Body."

Death of a Salesman swept through Broadway when it appeared in 1949. It won several awards and remains as one of the most important plays of the twentieth century.

Miller lived during the McCarthy era when Senator Joe McCarthy led a high-profile campaign against Communist sympathizers in the United States. His charge that Communists had infiltrated the government blew up into a full-scale inquisition of many state officials, politicians, entertainers, and writers. Miller was accused and immortalized the era in his play *The Crucible*, which compared the inquisitions to the seventeenth-century Salem witch trials.

WRITERS OF THE SOUTHERN GOTHIC

Horror and Humor

Who do you get when you combine the gothic horror of Edgar Allan Poe, the sardonic humor of Mark Twain, and the naturalism of Stephen Crane? You might very well get Flannery O'Connor, a Southern writer of the 1950s. You also get a new literary genre—Southern gothic.

SOUTHERN GOTHIC

Southern gothic came to prominence in the 1940s and 1950s when writers began using features of gothic storytelling to explore the state of Southern society. In the twentieth century, William Faulkner began developing a form of Southern gothic when he explored the decay of Southern traditions through mentally handicapped characters such as Benjy in *The Sound and the Fury*. Flannery O'Connor continued in the Southern gothic genre in her grotesque stories of the 1950s South.

The American gothic tradition had its beginnings with the dark romantics such as Nathaniel Hawthorne and Herman Melville, who used darker themes to raise questions about society and expose the dark side of the human heart. It continued with Edgar Allan Poe, who blended gothic elements with humor to explore themes like death. When it reached the twentieth century, it evolved into Southern gothic, where dramatic supernatural elements were replaced with more realistic, grotesque elements. These twisted forms came from the South's long legacy of racism, familial interbreeding and isolation, and madness.

Grotesque

The word *grotesque* means "comically distorted or ugly." As a literary term, grotesque is the use of a physical deformity for literary effect. The deformity usually focuses on the human body. A character might have a warped leg or, in more extreme cases like Kafka's Gregor Samsa in *The Metamorphosis*, be a combination human/animal. The blending of the familiar (the human body) and the unfamiliar (the deformity) is meant to incite disgust, maybe humor, but also empathy for the character and his or her plight. At the very least, the grotesque is meant to make you feel uncomfortable.

Characters of Southern gothic are usually deformed in some way or mentally unstable. The settings of Southern gothic stories and novels are broken-down, forgotten towns of the South. There is often violence, depravity, and a blurring of good and evil—one isn't sure whom to sympathize with. The complex characters, usually confused and looking for their place in society, highlight the darker aspects of the South. Southern gothic writers use these features to explore the problematic social order of the South, and expose its fragile structure.

FLANNERY O'CONNOR

Flannery O'Connor (1925–1964) was born to a prominent and devout Catholic family in Savannah, Georgia. Although O'Connor carried a strong personal faith, and themes of salvation and divine grace run throughout her work, she said her works explored Catholicism and faith with a "religious consciousness without religion"; that is, she avoided being dogmatic in her fiction (being overly dogmatic is usually a literary no-no).

O'Connor's stories are meant to knock you out of your seat: They're full of startling acts of violence that seem to come out of nowhere, abrupt endings, depraved and deformed characters, and freak accidents. Underlying all of her work is the humor of the grotesque.

Everything That Rises Must Converge

In the title story of one of her most famous short story collections, *Everything That Rises Must Converge* (1965), a young college graduate named Julian returns home to his mother, who requires an escort to her weekly YMCA class since she is still afraid to ride the bus after desegregation.

Evolution and Theology

The title of *Everything That Rises Must Converge* is a reference to a work by Pierre Teilhard de Chardin. De Chardin blended evolutionary theory and theology to develop a new theory of the "Omega Point"—a final pinnacle of consciousness toward which humans were evolving and that God had set into motion. "Remain true to yourself," he wrote, and "rise more ever upward toward greater consciousness and love . . . for everything that rises must converge."

Julian becomes increasingly annoyed at his mother's seemingly racist behavior on the bus. When his mother offers a coin to a black boy in an innocent (but condescending) gesture, Julian becomes furious (as does the boy's mother, who yells, "He don't take nobody's pennies!"). When Julian and his mother get off the bus, he scolds her for her behavior.

The story abruptly ends when his mother collapses to the pavement—her face distorted with one eye rolling back and one eye looking at him—in an apparent heart attack. O'Connor explained that in her work, startling acts of violence or brutality bring her characters "to reality and prepar[e] them to accept their moment of grace." Divine grace was an important theme in O'Connor's works.

Divine Grace

Divine grace is a theological concept that describes a divine force that enables humans to rise above themselves, resist temptation, and purify their souls.

Over her lifetime, O'Connor became a celebrated writer, producing three novels and thirty-two short stories. She died of lupus at the height of her career, when she was only thirty-nine years old.

CARSON MCCULLERS

Carson McCullers (1917–1967) was a short-story writer from Columbus, Georgia. Her eccentric, displaced characters living on the fringes of society earned her a place in the Southern gothic pantheon. Her most well-known work, *The Heart Is a Lonely Hunter* (1940), is about a pair of deaf-mutes living in the South. They are innocent, handicapped figures looking for a place in society.

EUDORA WELTY

Though she would have hated the term (she hated labels), Eudora Welty (1909–2001) is also considered a Southern gothic writer. She was a short-story writer and novelist whose works emphasized human beings' connection to place, in her case, the South. She won the Pulitzer Prize in 1973 for her novel *The Optimist's Daughter*.

CORMAC MCCARTHY

Cormac McCarthy (1933–), a contemporary author, is continuing the Southern gothic tradition with his work. His books such as the Border Trilogy novels and *The Road* contain violent, sinister characters and explore themes of isolation and immorality in places like the Southwest and the Mexico–U.S. border. For McCarthy, the old cowboy narrative gets a bleaker, more twisted redo.

Chapter 8

Contemporary American Literature and Beyond

Contemporary American literature is usually defined as literature written from 1945 on, the year after which it becomes too soon to define literary movements and too soon to determine whose work will endure after the dust settles.

What *has* become clear is that the work that has been produced over these years is diverse: a rich patchwork of voices, perspectives, and styles that reflect the diversity of American culture. Whitman described himself and his home city of New York as containing "multitudes"; America and its literature can be described by the same term—American literature contains "multitudes," each adding a distinct contribution to the end result.

In the 1950s through the 1970s, writers began to blur the lines between fact and fiction in works that explored crime and pop culture. Truman Capote, Tom Wolfe, and Norman Mailer all contributed to new forms like the nonfiction novel and New Journalism. The middle class became a dominant theme, as America became more suburban and people began feeling more stifled. Magical realism—a literary technique that blends fact and fiction, fantasy and reality, first established by Latin writers—made its way into American fiction.

Finally, another literary movement opened up in the first few decades after the end of the wars: Postmodernism came to describe the writers whose works experimented with narration, the authority of the author, the relationship between text and reader, and other elements that made up the "normal" mode of storytelling. Postmodernists questioned almost everything—right down to the nature of meaning itself.

Writers are continuing to play with the boundaries of form, and put themselves on the frontier of new themes. Let's see what writers have been up to over the past half century and beyond.

TODAY'S LITERATURE

Postmodernism in Turmoil

In many ways, contemporary American literature is a coming-of-age story as writers trace the experience of assimilation in the melting pot of America. Multicultural writing has become a dominant theme over the past half century as writers trace their journey and write about what it means to be American. Here's a rundown of the most dominant writers and themes.

JEWISH-AMERICAN LITERATURE

Jewish-American literature began to take shape in the 1950s with Saul Bellow's masterful stories that navigated conflicts of Jewish-American identity with the modern era. Jewish-American literature highlights the alienation and loneliness that underlie assimilation, and the humor, endurance, and grit necessary for survival.

Saul Bellow

Saul Bellow (1915–2005) is one of the most decorated writers of the twentieth century. He won the National Book Award three times, a Pulitzer Prize, and was awarded the Nobel Prize in Literature in 1976. An immigrant from Canada, Bellow emphasized education and achievement as a moral responsibility and a way out of suffering. In his novel *The Adventures of Augie March* (1953), the title character, naturally intelligent, fails to make a commitment to education, choosing to float through life instead. Karl Ragnar Gierow, of the Swedish Academy, in his Nobel Prize Presentation Speech for Bellow, cited Bellow's work for its "penetrating insight into the outer and inner complications that drive us to act, or prevent us from acting, and that can be called the dilemma of our age."

Philip Roth

Philip Roth's (1933-) novels explore the journey of assimilation Jewish Americans took after the world wars—how their identity is defined, changed, and complicated by memories of the Holocaust during the prosperity of the postwar years. Roth can be provocative—in some cases Jews become the victims of other Jews, as he shows how easily people play into stereotypes. The relationships between reality and fiction, between the author and the text, are flexible in his work. Nathan Zuckerman, the protagonist of several of his novels, who also serves as Roth's alter ego, becomes a figure through which Roth explores his own relationship to his books (this is a feature of metafiction, another feature of postmodern novels).

The Holocaust

By the end of the war in 1945, more than 6 million Eastern European Jews had been systematically killed by Hitler's regime.

Elie Wiesel

Elie Wiesel (1928-2016) survived one of the worst crises of humanity—the Holocaust. Only Wiesel and his two older sisters survived when Nazi soldiers took him and his family from their village in Romania to a concentration camp. Devastated, Wiesel lost his belief in God. He gathered his strength to make an account of the atrocities he witnessed, publishing *Night* in 1958. The work describes the humiliation, shame, and guilt Wiesel felt as he watched his father and his people get annihilated. Wiesel dedicated his life to speaking and working on behalf of all people who are persecuted, and he won the Nobel Peace Prize in 1986.

CONTEMPORARY AFRICAN-AMERICAN LITERATURE

At the heart of much of contemporary African-American literature is the question of how to move forward from the pain of the past and the racial discrimination that still exists. Is it through militant anger or peaceful resistance? Is it through a reshaping of African tradition or complete assimilation? The works of African-American literature of the past seventy years are vibrant and passionate works of protest, witness, and power.

Ralph Ellison

Ralph Ellison (1914–1994) created an alternative black protagonist to Richard Wright's Bigger in *Native Son*. The narrator of Ellison's *Invisible Man* is educated, self-aware, and sophisticated—and he doesn't have a name. When Ellison published his modernist novel *Invisible Man* in 1952, he became one of America's most important African-American writers. He also became one its most controversial figures for presenting a picture of African-American culture that focused less on the victimization of blacks and more on the complex forces—black and white—that made him "invisible." For Ellison, the way to freedom is through embracing one's culture, not condemning it. He presented African-American culture as rich with traditions, rituals, and a source of identity, something to be embraced.

James Baldwin

James Baldwin (1924–1987) recalled feeling lost in his circumstances of being a poor young black man in Harlem: "I knew I was black, of course, but I also knew I was smart. I didn't know how I would use my mind, or even if I could, but that was the only thing I had to use." His passionate fictionalized autobiography of his struggles, *Go Tell It on the Mountain* (1953), has become a classic of African-American literature. Like Ellison, Baldwin emphasized the power of community rather than the propagation of divisive aggression. And like Ellison, he was bitterly criticized for it. Baldwin became an early spokesman for the civil rights movement.

Toni Morrison

In 1993, Toni Morrison (1931–) became the first African-American woman to win the Nobel Prize in Literature. A master storyteller, Morrison's novels explore racial conflict and identity across ages. She writes, "In so many earlier books by African-American writers, particularly the men, I felt that they were not writing to me. But what interested me was the African-American experience throughout whichever time I spoke of. It was always about African-American culture and people—good, bad, indifferent, whatever—but that was, for me, the universe." One of her greatest works, *Beloved* (1987), is about Sethe, a former slave who makes a horrific decision to kill her children rather than see them back in captivity. Her books are brave and powerful.

Henry Dumas

Dubbed an "absolute genius" by Toni Morrison, Henry Dumas was an African-American poet. His collection of poetry, *Play Ebony, Play Ivory*, was published posthumously in 1974. Dumas was shot on a New York City subway platform by transit police in 1968. It's still unclear what happened during this incident. Dumas was only thirty-three years old.

CONTEMPORARY AMERICAN INDIAN LITERATURE

In 1983, critic Kenneth Lincoln coined the term "Native American Renaissance" to refer to the works produced by Native Americans from the 1960s onward. American Indians and scholars have been reclaiming their oral traditions using the English language and capturing their experiences in the language of their enslavers. Lincoln pinpointed the beginning of the movement with the work of the author N. Scott Momaday.

N. Scott Momaday

N. Scott Momaday (1934–), a Kiowa Indian writer, was born in Oklahoma and has spent his life straddling mainstream culture (he is a professor at Stanford University) and life on reservations. Momaday's works emphasize the power of imagination and myth in shaping identity. He writes, "We are what we imagine. Our very existence consists in our imagination of ourselves. Our best destiny is to imagine, at least, completely, who and what, and that we are."

His novel, *House Made of Dawn* (1969), draws from his experiences, including his life in Navajo and San Carlos Apache communities. The novel won the Pulitzer Prize for Fiction.

Louise Erdrich

Louise Erdrich (1954–) was born to a Chippewa mother and a German-American father. Her parents encouraged her to write—they paid her a nickel for every story she wrote and collected them into small books for her to keep. Erdrich's early life was rich with her mother's stories, many of which ended up in her novels. Her novel *Love Medicine* won the National Book Critics Circle Award in 1984. Erdrich's stories tell about issues with family, human sexuality, and identity among full- and mix-blood American Indians.

Native American or Indian?

People often wonder which term to use—Native American or American Indian. At an international conference in Geneva in 1977, natives unanimously decided that the term American Indian was preferable. As noted American Indian actor and activist Russell Means said, "We were enslaved as American Indians, we were colonized as American Indians, and we will gain our freedom as American Indians—and then we will call ourselves any damn thing we choose."

LATINO-AMERICAN LITERATURE

Latino-American literature is a relatively new field, but it has grown quickly. Latino-American literature speaks of bridging cultures and assimilation.

Sandra Cisneros

Perhaps the most visible Latino-American writer is Sandra Cisneros (1954–). Her acclaimed first novel, *The House on Mango Street* (1984), is a staple of classrooms across America. Her vivid story of a young Latina girl growing up in Chicago blends humor and charm to discuss serious topics like female sexuality and identity. Cisneros writes, "I think I was put on the planet to tell these stories. Use what you know to help heal the pain in your community. We've got to tell our own history."

Bildungsroman

Cisneros's *The House on Mango Street* is an example of a *bildungsroman*, a literary genre in which a protagonist comes of age during the course of the story (the word is a German literary term). The psychological, emotional, and physical changes that the character undergoes are a key feature of the genre.

Julia Alvarez

Julia Alvarez (1950–) is a Dominican-American poet and novelist. Her first novel, *How the García Girls Lost Their Accents* (1991), discusses the Latina immigration and the challenges of cultural integration. The highly personal novel describes how four sisters negotiate their place in New York City culture after emigrating from the Dominican Republic. Language and its ability to bind and separate individuals from their identity is a theme of Alvarez's work.

Richard Rodriguez

Richard Rodriguez (1944–) is another Latino-American writer who explores language in the context of Latino-American culture.

His writings investigate the separation between parent and child that language can create once the child learns the new language of his adoptive country. Because of his experiences, Rodriguez has become an outspoken figure on bilingual education, arguing that total immersion is a more beneficial and effective way of integrating children than bilingual education.

Junot Díaz

Junot Díaz (1968–) is a Dominican-American writer, currently teaching creative writing at the Massachusetts Institute of Technology (MIT). He received the Pulitzer Prize for Fiction for his novel *The Brief Wondrous Life of Oscar Wao* (2007). His works explore masculinity and Dominican identity in America.

ASIAN-AMERICAN LITERATURE

Asian-American literature is another relatively new but rapidly expanding field. New, strong voices are published every year. Writers such as Jhumpa Lahiri have begun to capture the Indian-American immigrant experience and expand the field, as writers like Chang-rae Lee have continued to document the painful experience of assimilation that writers like Maxine Hong Kingston and Amy Tan documented in the seventies and eighties.

Maxine Hong Kingston

Maxine Hong Kingston (1940–) is a Chinese-American writer. In her memoir *The Woman Warrior* (1976), she blends myth, fable, and fact to explore gender and ethnicity in her life as young Chinese-American immigrant growing up in California. Her narrator asks an important question at the center of many contemporary novels exploring cultural identity: "Chinese-Americans, when you try to understand what things in you are Chinese, how do you separate what is peculiar to childhood, to poverty, insanities, one family, your mother who marked your growing with stories, from what is Chinese? What is Chinese tradition and what is the movies?"

Tripmaster Monkey

In 1989, Kingston published a book called *Tripmaster Monkey: His Fake Book*, a twentieth-century odyssey set in the bohemian era of 1960s San Francisco. The book's protagonist is Wittman Ah Sing, a reference to Walt Whitman. Kingston combines the East and West to exaggerate the "Americanness" of the characters.

Amy Tan

Amy Tan (1952–) is one of the most popular Chinese-American writers working today. Her novel *The Joy Luck Club* (1989) has been translated into twenty-five languages and was made into a box-office hit (Oliver Stone served as executive producer, and Tan cowrote the screenplay). Tan came to writing late—she didn't publish her first novel until she was thirty-seven, after she took up writing to escape the boredom of her freelance writing job. The novel tells the story of four Asian women who escape China to come to America in the 1940s and the strain that develops between them and their Americanized daughters.

NEW FORMS AND NEW THEMES

Literature for a New Age

America is the land of experimentation. Let's see what's been cooking over the past seventy years in the American literary world as writers continue to expand and change literary forms and themes for the new age.

NEW FORM: THE NONFICTION NOVEL AND "NEW JOURNALISM"

One of the most exciting new forms to come out of the second half of the twentieth century is the nonfiction novel. In a nonfiction novel, all of the details are true, but they are shaped using literary techniques of fiction writing. This blend of fact and fictional technique allows the writer a greater range of expression than simple reporting and storytelling.

At first, people considered the nonfiction novel to be the last resort of a fatigued novelist reaching a failure of imagination. Instead, the form proved to be a rich source of creativity for a diverse group of major writers. Let's explore how the form played out in the works of three important writers.

CAPOTE'S TRIUMPH

Truman Capote (1924–1984) ushered in the nonfiction novel in America with his work, *In Cold Blood*. The book told the story of the brutal murder of the Clutter family in Kansas and the execution of their two killers, Perry Smith and Richard Hickock. Truman Capote spent six years meticulously researching the book, interviewing family members, neighbors, and even the killers. In fact, over the course of writing the book, he famously became friends with the killers.

Above all, Capote was intent on creating a "factually immaculate" piece. The book created a huge sensation when it was published—the *New York Times* hailed it a masterpiece, and Capote's fame was secured.

So what drove Capote to spend six years researching a (unfortunately) common murder story miles away in Kansas? He explains (from "The Story Behind a Nonfiction Novel" by George Plimpton, published in book form in *Truman Capote: Conversations*):

> The story was brief, just several paragraphs stating the facts: A Mr. Herbert W. Clutter, who had served on the Farm Credit Board during the Eisenhower Administration, his wife and two teen-aged children, had been brutally, entirely mysteriously, murdered on a lonely wheat and cattle ranch in a remote part of Kansas. There was nothing really exceptional about it; one reads items concerning multiple murders many times in the course of a year. . . . after reading the story it suddenly struck me that a crime, the study of one such, might provide the broad scope I needed to write the kind of book I wanted to write. Moreover, the human heart being what it is, murder was a theme not likely to darken and yellow with time.

Harper Lee

Capote was not alone writing *In Cold Blood*: He had significant help from his childhood friend, Harper Lee. Capote and Lee both grew up in Monroeville, Alabama, bonding over their difficult home lives and social awkwardness. Truman was ridiculed for being effeminate, and Lee, stronger than most, defended him. Lee went with Capote to Kansas to work with him on the story of the Clutter murders and remained by his side for months, helping him build the story. Her easygoing personality helped win over locals, and she was able to collect information and conduct interviews that Capote otherwise had a hard time getting. In 1960, Lee published her own novel, *To Kill a Mockingbird*. The coming-of-age story about a girl named Scout and her attorney father's attempt to secure a fair trial for a black man who is charged with raping a white woman has become a cornerstone work about racism in the South. The book won a Pulitzer Prize and continues to sell millions of copies a year.

Other Blends of Fact and Fiction

In Capote's version of the nonfiction novel, he leaves himself completely out of the narration. There is almost no trace of a narrator in the book—he tried very hard to present the book as an objective piece of literary work. Other writers began to expand the nonfiction novel and take it into new directions, experimenting with narration and adding layers of subjectivity.

GONZO JOURNALISM

Hunter S. Thompson (1937–2005) developed a writing style called gonzo journalism, which mixed his own reflections and experiences into the work. Thompson acts as "reporter" but doesn't pretend that the work is an objective presentation of factual events. It should also be pointed out that the reporter, Thompson, who appears on the printed page isn't necessarily the same person as Thompson in real life.

New Journalism

In a similar vein to Capote's *In Cold Blood* and gonzo journalism, another blending of nonfiction/fiction appeared, dubbed New Journalism. Tom Wolfe (1931–) pioneered the form in his collected essays, *The Kandy-Kolored Tangerine-Flake Streamline Baby* (1965). New Journalism was a form of personal and subjective "creative" reporting. When asked of his opinion of New Journalism, Capote said, uncharitably (from *Truman Capote: Conversations*), "It's useless for a writer whose talent is essentially journalistic to attempt creative reportage, because it simply won't work. . . . to be a good creative reporter, you have to be a very good fiction writer."

MAILER'S TRIUMPH

Norman Mailer's (1923–2007) *The Executioner's Song* became the most decorated form of New Journalism when it was awarded the Pulitzer Prize for Fiction in 1980. Perhaps the most emotional example from the genre, Mailer's portrayal of the events of a volatile and troubled killer, Gary Gilmore, and his acceptance and dignity at his execution is tragic and moving.

NEW THEME: THE MIDDLE CLASS

The middle class became a prominent theme of fiction during the 1960s and through the 1980s as America turned more suburban and the deadening effects of holding down a job, maintaining a marriage, raising kids, and chasing possessions began to take hold. The writer

John Updike (1932–2009) captured the trials of middle-class life in his popular Rabbit books, beginning with *Rabbit, Run* in 1960.

When asked why he chose the middle class as a subject, Updike said, "I like middles. It is in the middles that extremes clash, where ambiguity restlessly rules." Updike came from the middle class—he was born in Pennsylvania to a teacher and a writer.

Updike's Rabbit books follow Harry "Rabbit" Angstrom, a middle-class everyman and Updike's alter ego. The four novels follow Angstrom through the 1950s to the 1990s. Over the course of the novels Angstrom goes through a midlife crisis, relives the Vietnam War, and settles into old age.

John Cheever

Another chronicler of the middle class is John Cheever (1912–1982). Cheever's novels and stories explored the trappings of suburban professional life. Check out his short-story collection *The Way Some People Live* (1943).

Magical Realism

Realism has had a long history in American literature—dating back to Mark Twain and William Dean Howells. In the twentieth century it took a turn toward the "magical," influenced most notably by the works of Latin-American writers such as Gabriel García Márquez (who won the Nobel Prize in Literature in 1982) and Isabel Allende.

So what is magical realism? It is a presentation of magical or unreal features in a realistic context. In Márquez's version of magical realism, things happen like angels falling to earth—and no one in the story questions the reality of this. This seamless blend of fantasy and reality allows writers to explore realities that exist outside of mainstream culture (and therefore alternative views) in an otherwise safe context.

Magical realism snuck its way into American literature in the twentieth and twenty-first centuries as well, taking a cue from Márquez. The writer Junot Díaz features old curses and magical mongooses in his novel *The Brief Wondrous Life of Oscar Wao,* and the writer Jonathan Safran Foer uses magical realism to explore the Jewish diaspora in his novel *Everything Is Illuminated* (2002).

Postmodernism

Postmodernism is a whole other beast that could take an entire chapter to explore. Let's take a brief look at what it is in the context of American literature. Generally, postmodernism describes much of the work that came after the modernists. and anything that inveighed against the modernists and their way of thinking.

While modernism sought a departure from classical and traditional forms, postmodernism rebelled against modernism and questioned the very idea of truth, playing with and disturbing the lines between author and text, between high art and popular culture.

Writers such as Roth and Updike created alter egos to explore their relationships to the text, blurring the line between author and text. To beautiful effect, Tim O'Brien does this in his novel *The Things They Carried.* The novel explores a soldier's account of his war experience. O'Brien explores the nature of storytelling and the truth in his novel, and in some cases his "versions" of the truth are truer than what happened. More recently, the author David Foster Wallace wrote works that experimented with storytelling methods, using footnotes and endnotes to continuously call out and question realities in the text, a key function of postmodernism. His novel

Infinite Jest is considered by many critics to be one of the best English-language novels of the twentieth century.

Thomas Pynchon

Thomas Pynchon (1937–) is another writer whose highly self-conscious style is a good example of postmodernism literature. Check out *Gravity's Rainbow*, which won the National Book Award for Fiction in 1974.

Other Forms and Themes

Here's a quick rundown of some of the highlights of the past few decades:

- **Technology:** With the rise of the digital age, technology has become an even more dominant theme in literature and has expanded the science-fiction genre. The terms "cyberpunk" and "postcyberpunk" have come to define genres that explore the role of informational technology in culture. Check out novels by William Gibson (*Neuromancer, Pattern Recognition*) and Neal Stephenson (*Snow Crash, Cryptonomicon*) to see the exciting ways these fields are taking shape.
- **Apocalyptic fiction:** Seems like at the end of every century, everyone thinks the world is going to end. Apocalyptic literature is as old as the Bible, but see where writers like Cormac McCarthy (*The Road*) have taken apocalyptic fiction at the close of the twentieth century.
- **Memoir and historical fiction:** People like other people. People like history. Put these two things together and you get a rich array of works of memoir and historical fiction in the late twentieth and

early twenty-first centuries. Film and television have made these genres even more popular as they're often used as springboards for television series and movies.

Authors such as E.L. Doctorow and William Kennedy are known primarily for their historical fiction but also saw successful film (and Broadway) adaptations of their work. Doctorow's *Ragtime* made it on *Time* magazine's All-Time 100 Best Novels list, the movie version (with Norman Mailer acting in a small part) was nominated for eight Oscars, and the Broadway musical adaptation won four Tony Awards. Kennedy's *Ironweed* is on the Modern Library's 100 Best Novels of the English language, won the Pulitzer Prize, and the movie version (featuring Jack Nicholson and Meryl Streep) was nominated for four Oscars.

More recently, Elizabeth Gilbert has tackled both memoir and historical fiction. Her memoir *Eat, Pray, Love* was a *New York Times* bestseller and successful movie featuring Julia Roberts, and her 2013 book *The Signature of All Things*, set in the century of Darwin, "entwines the historic and the imagined so subtly as to read like good nonfiction," according to a review by Barbara Kingsolver in the *New York Times*.

Of course, more forms and themes are developing all the time (and will continue to). Keep reading, folks!

INDEX